ALL ABOUT
THE ANGELS

"See that you despise not one of these little ones: for I say to you, that their angels in heaven always see the face of my Father who is in heaven."

—Matthew 18:10

H. Hofmann

The Flight into Egypt.

ALL ABOUT THE ANGELS

by

Fr. Paul O'Sullivan, O.P.
[E.D.M.]

" . . .he hath given his angels charge
over thee, and in their hands shall they
bear thee up, lest perhaps thou dash thy
foot against a stone."

—Matthew 4:6

TAN BOOKS AND PUBLISHERS, INC.
Rockford, Illinois 61105

CUM PERMISSU SUPERIORUM.

ISBN: 0-89555-388-0

Library of Congress Catalog Card No.: 90-70122

Printed and bound in the United States of America.

TAN BOOKS AND PUBLISHERS, INC.
P.O. Box 424
Rockford, Illinois 61105

1990

A truly beautiful book—

It opens up a new and glorious world
*   to its readers;*
It gives them a happiness and joy
*   they never had before;*
It is a book for all, priests and people,
*   young and old.*

APOSTOLIC NUNCIATURE
LISBON, PORTUGAL

Dear Father Paul O'Sullivan,

Many thanks for sending me the beautiful little book on the Angels which you have just published.

It comes at a most opportune moment, for in the present state of unrest and suffering in the world no better remedy can be found than the all-powerful protection of God's glorious Angels.

The doctrine of Holy Church on these Blessed Spirits is most consoling and should be thoroughly understood by all Christians.

The Angels are our best friends, and you tell your readers all about them in a manner so clear and interesting that the perusal of your book will certainly awaken a great love for and confidence in these glorious Princes of Heaven. In return, the Angels will obtain for us many graces and deliver us from many evils.

I remain with the highest esteem,

Yours very sincerely,

✠ *Peter Ciriaci, Apostolic Nuncio*

1 September 1945

Publisher's Note

All About the Angels is one of the best-loved books of Fr. Paul O'Sullivan, O.P. All of Fr. O'Sullivan's works, in fact, have been favorites of Catholic readers for many years.

These books used to be published in Portugal, starting in the 1940's, and we found them to be very popular in the 1970's when we were importing them from there. In the meantime, however, the Portuguese publisher has ceased publishing these books, and St. Martin Apostolate in Dublin, a Dominican organization, has been distributing them.

We are very pleased to have been given permission to republish Fr. O'Sullivan's books. They are short, easy to understand and full of beautiful and encouraging stories from our Catholic heritage. They are conceived and written to help us live our Catholic Faith on an everyday basis in a full, rich, rewarding manner, so that we may reap both the happiness and peace in this world and the eternal salvation of our souls in the next that come from doing God's holy will. Fr. O'Sullivan was obviously convinced that it was not so hard to become a saint—if we will only make use of the means Christ has put at our disposal in the Catholic Religion—and he has set out to show us the way.

We hope that *All About the Angels* will be more popular than ever in this new edition. And we trust that it will increase faith in and devotion to the blessed angelic spirits, present invisibly all around us—the Angels, who are ever eager to help us and to lead us to our heavenly home.

—The Publishers
January 12, 1990

CONTENTS

Foreword

WHY IGNORE OUR BEST FRIENDS?

"Make friends with the Angels" is the advice which the great Pope, St. Leo, gives every Christian and it is advice that everyone should follow.

If we make friends with the Angels—and nothing is easier—we shall receive innumerable and great favors which otherwise we shall never obtain. Our Angel friends, too, will shield and protect us from countless dangers, evils, sickness and accidents which, without their help, we could not possibly avoid. In a word, these all-powerful and loving protectors will secure for us a degree of happiness that, without their assistance, we could not hope for in this vale of tears!

Another reason we should make friends with the Angels is that they are our dearest and best friends. A good friend, a friend who is able and always ready to help us, a friend to whom we can have recourse in all our troubles and sorrows, is one of the greatest blessings God can give us. Our human hearts thirst for love and sympathy.

Among men we rarely or never find such a friend, but this is not so with the Angels. They are most desirous to be our friends and they love us with all the intensity of their angelic natures.

Since they are all-powerful and generous, we can have the fullest confidence in their help and friendship.

The one friendship on this Earth that gives us any idea of the love of the Angels is the affection of a mother. This is the purest, the most generous, the strongest of all human loves. The mother loves her children with unbounded affection.

God has placed in the mother's heart an instinct of love so great that it almost borders on the supernatural. She forgets herself and thinks only of her children. She works for them, sacrifices herself for them, and gives them her all. If one of them should fall sick or be plunged into some great sorrow, to that one she devotes a more special gentleness and a more loving care.

We sometimes see a frail woman watch by the bedside of her sick child — eating little, resting little, consumed with a poignant anxiety — for ten, twenty or even thirty days, never complaining, and never faltering. When these days of anguish and bitterness are past, this almost superhuman effort, these long, weary vigils, seem to have cost her nothing. The mother's love sustained her. Yet, strong men who lose their sleep for two or three consecutive nights complain that they find it hard to work the following day.

If a poor frail mother — she may be young or old, rich or poor, full of weaknesses and imperfections — can rise to such a height of love and abnegation as this, what may we not expect from God's Angels, who have no defects, no imperfections and who love us with all the mighty power of their glorious angelic natures?

The teaching of the Church about the Angels is most beautiful and consoling, but unfortunately many Christians have scant knowledge of the great world of the Angels. They know little about these blessed Spirits, love them little and seldom pray to them. Worst of all, *they do not realize their presence.* They show no confidence in them, and they do not call on them for help when dangers and difficulties press around.

As a result they forfeit a thousand blessings that they might easily enjoy and fall victim to a thousand accidents that they might easily have avoided.

HOW COMES IT THAT THE ANGELS ARE SO LITTLE KNOWN AND SO LITTLE LOVED?

Simply because many, whose duty it is to teach this most important doctrine are gravely negligent in fulfilling their obligation.

First of all, Christian Mothers should instill deeply into the minds of their children a clear, vivid and abiding sense of the presence of their dear Angels.

It is not sufficient to give them vague, hazy, insufficient notions of these Blessed Spirits, nor is it enough to teach them to say a short prayer at morning and at night to their Angel Guardians.

They should devote much time and much attention to this all-important subject. Children

must be taught constantly from their tenderest
years to have a real love and friendship for their
Angels, to have boundless confidence in them.
They must be accustomed to feel and realize the
personal presence of their Angels, to call on them
in all their fears and troubles.

How much better this would be than that the
children should have their heads filled with fool-
ish fear of ghosts and hobgoblins as so frequently
happens.

Mothers who impress on their children this
great lesson confer on them inestimable blessings during all the long years of their lives.

On the other hand, if they neglect this duty
or make light of it, they do a great wrong to their
dear ones for they deprive them of the best and
most powerful friends.

Catechists, too, and teachers of the young in
schools, colleges and convents are frequently re-
miss in teaching those in their charge all about
the blessed Angels. The minds of their pupils are
developing, and the teaching of the mothers in
the home, no matter how good it might have been,
must be perfected and developed.

Professors of older students, boys and girls, are
perhaps greater offenders. They rarely mention
the subject of the Angels in their classes. Why?
Do not the Angels exist? Are they not our best
friends? Is there not much to be said about them?

Priests of course can do much to remedy the
neglect of parents and teachers by preaching at
times on the Angels, by wise counsels in the con-

fessional and by exhorting the faithful to read books on the Angels.

Priests who do so receive most striking graces.

THE OBJECT OF THIS BOOK

There are few books published about the Angels, and these few are mostly doctrinal and abstruse. They do not appeal to the general public and fail to create in the heart of the ordinary reader that love and trust which they ought to have in the Angels.

It is so different in the case of the Saints. There are innumerable books attractively written about these great servants of God which help us to know them, to love them and follow their example.

There are also pictures of all kinds, large and small, of the Saints which we hang on our walls, place on our work tables or use in our prayer-books. We thus live, as it were, in the presence and company of the Saints.

Pictures of the Angels are few and to a certain extent misleading because the Angel is, as a rule, represented as guiding little children; whereas, adults should, with equal reason, be reminded of their Angels and have suitable pictures of them.

In the Sacred Scriptures Angels are pictured as helping Abraham and Jacob, Elias and Daniel, Agar and Judith, Peter and Paul—all adults.

The object of these pages is to awaken in the hearts of our readers a real love and friendship for the Holy Angels, an abiding confidence in them, and *above all* to make readers realize and feel vividly the presence of these loving Spirits ever by their sides.

OUR PLAN

At the cost of inverting the natural order of our book, we will commence by relating some of the modern and best authenticated apparitions of Angels. We do this, first of all, to stimulate the interest of our readers and secondly because many seem to think that angelic apparitions are a thing of the past.

We shall then, following the doctrine of St. Thomas, tell our readers all about the Angels, who they are, what they are doing, where they are, how beautiful, how lovable, how powerful, how eager they are to help us and what great advantages we gain by honoring and loving these great princes of Heaven.

Next we will recall some of the beautiful stories of the Angels which we find in the Scriptures, in the lives of the Martyrs and other Saints.

In the course of our book we quote striking and well-authenticated incidents from the lives of men and women, boys and girls living in the world like ourselves. These facts have a special value, as they go to show how ready the dear Angels are to help, not only saints, but all who love them, no matter how modest these may be.

We humbly ask the dear Angels to help us in this work of love.

Chapter 1

THE APPARITIONS OF
THE ANGEL GUARDIAN OF
PORTUGAL IN THE YEAR 1916

We cannot begin our little book on the Angels better than by giving an accurate and authoritative account of the apparitions of the Guardian Angel of Portugal, in Fatima. These are perhaps the most striking and best authenticated angelic apparitions of modern times.

Portugal has received many and great blessings during the long years of her history. To mention a few: She was for many centuries one of the greatest Catholic nations in the world, we might perhaps say the greatest. She discovered and conquered half the present-known world in less than one hundred years, which was certainly a wonderful feat. But she did more. She Christianized her vast empire with a care and humanity that has never been surpassed. The best authorities bear witness to this fact, and the Church has fully recognized it by granting many notable privileges to the Catholics of Portugal, privileges which they still continue to enjoy.

A second great favor was the extraordinary devotion to the Blessed Sacrament which gives her

1

a claim to the glorious title of "the Land of the Eucharist."

A third outstanding grace bestowed on this favored country was the exceptional love and devotion to Our Blessed Lady which began with the first king of Portugal and was continued by his successors, who held themselves bound to insist on and maintain the solemn consecration of the realm to Mary Immaculate, whom they chose for their Patroness and Protectress. Later on, kings offered the royal crown to Mary, so that for long years the kings of Portugal never wore the royal diadem.

The crowning grace, however, was reserved for our own days, when in May 1917 and the following five months, God's Holy Mother appeared in Fatima, establishing there one of the most glorious Marian sanctuaries in the world.

An outstanding feature of these apparitions and one that none other of her sanctuaries can claim is the appearance of the Angel Guardian of Portugal in 1916, the year preceding the apparitions.

The glorious Archangel appeared on three occasions and in three different places to the privileged children who were destined to see Our Lady. He taught them how to pray and sanctify themselves, assuring them that Jesus and Mary had special designs for them, thus preparing them for the coming of God's Holy Mother the following year, 1917.

The following is an exact account of these angelic apparitions.

THE FIRST VISION OF THE ANGEL

The eldest of the three children to whom Our Lady appeared, now known as Sister Lucy, tells us in her own simple language how the Angel of Portugal appeared three times to her and her cousins, Jacinta and Francisco.

She did not remember the exact dates of these apparitions, for she says, "At that time I made no account of months or weeks or days." She was an uncultured little peasant girl.

"It was sometime in the Spring of 1916 that Jacinta, Francis and I were minding our sheep in a place called Chousa Velha. It was in the morning and a light rain-like dew began to fall as we went up the side of the hill with our sheep, looking for a rock [or] some place where we could shelter ourselves from the rain. In the midst of an olive grove we found a cave, which we entered for the first time. When the rain had cleared off, we still lingered there some time, ate our lunch and said our Rosary. After this we began to play with some stones.

"Suddenly, though the day was very mild, a strong wind began to sway the branches of the tree and we glanced up to see the cause of it.

"We saw over the trees a light as white as snow and in the midst of it the form of a young man as brilliant as crystal as when it is lit up by the light of the sun. As he approached us, we began to see his features clearly. We were surprised, absorbed by what we saw, but [we] said not a word.

"On coming near us he said, *'Don't be afraid, I am the Angel of Peace. Pray with me.'*

"Then kneeling on the ground, he bent his head low and we, moved by a supernatural inspiration, imitated him and repeated the words that we heard him say:

"*'My God, I believe, I adore, I hope in Thee and I love Thee.'*

"*'I ask Thee to pardon those who do not believe, adore, hope in and love Thee.'*

"After saying these words three times, he arose and said to us: *'Pray thus. The hearts of Jesus and Mary are listening to the voice of your supplications.'* He then disappeared.

"The supernatural feeling that had taken possession of us was so intense that we did not even think of our own existence; we remained for a long time as the Angel had left us, repeating over and over the same prayer.

"We felt the presence of God so overpowering and so intimate in our souls that we did not even dare to speak of it among ourselves. Next day we still felt the same intense feeling of God's presence, which only after the lapse of some time began to lessen. We did not think of speaking of the apparition nor did we make any agreement to keep it secret; the apparition itself seemed to impose silence on us; we did not say a word about it.

"Perhaps it made more impression on us as it was the first apparition which we had had."

THE SECOND VISION OF THE ANGEL

"The second vision of the Angel was in the heat of summer. We went to pass the hour of the great heat of the day in the shade of some trees, in a place called Arneiro.

"Suddenly we saw the same Angel near us.

"He said: *'What are you doing? Pray. Pray much.*
"'The Hearts of Jesus and Mary have special designs of mercy on you. Offer constantly to the Most High prayers and sacrifices.'
"'What sacrifices?' I asked.
"'Offer a sacrifice of everything you can in reparation for the sins which offend Him and in supplication for the conversion of sinners. Obtain for our country peace. I am the Guardian Angel of Portugal.
"'Above all accept and bear with resignation the sufferings Our Lord will send you.'

"These words of the Angel engraved themselves on our hearts like a light which made us see who God was, how He loved us and how He wished us to love Him. It made us understand the value of sacrifice, how pleasing it is to God and how He converts sinners by means of it.

"Therefore, from that moment we began to offer to God everything that mortified us or caused us pain, without seeking to do other penances, except indeed, to repeat for hours, prostrate on the earth, the prayer the Angel had taught us."

THE THIRD VISION OF THE ANGEL

"The third vision was at the end of October or beginning of November, for as I have said, I did not in those days make account of days or weeks.

"This third vision took place in an olive grove called Pregueira belonging to my parents. We had said our Rosary and the prayer that the Angel had taught us in the first vision.

"He now appeared to us with a chalice in his hand and over it a Host from which drops of Blood fell into the Chalice.

"Leaving the Chalice and the Host suspended in the air, he prostrated himself on the earth and repeated the following prayer three times: *'Most Holy Trinity, Father, Son and Holy Ghost, I adore Thee profoundly and offer Thee the most Precious Body, Blood, Soul and Divinity of Jesus Christ, present in all the tabernacles of the world, in reparation for all the outrages, sacrileges, and indifference with which He is offended. And by the infinite merits of His most Sacred Heart and the Immaculate Heart of Mary [I] ask Thee for the conversion of poor sinners.'*

"He then arose and again took the chalice. To me he gave the Host and to Jacinta and Francisco he gave what was in the chalice, saying: *'Take and drink the Body and Blood of Jesus Christ, horribly outraged by ungrateful men. Make reparation for their crimes and console our God.'*

"Once more he prostrated himself on the earth and repeated three times the same prayer: *'Most*

Holy Trinity, etc...' and disappeared.

"Overcome by supernatural emotion, we imitated the Angel and did all that he had done. The feeling of the Divine Presence overcame us and, as it were, annihilated us completely. It seemed to deprive us of the use of our corporal senses for a long time. During these days we performed our material actions as if impelled by this supernatural force. The peace and happiness which we enjoyed were great and intimate, our souls were completely wrapt up in God. The physical weakness we felt was also great.

"The apparitions of Our Blessed Lady later on produced different effects on us. We enjoyed the same intimate joy, peace and happiness, but instead of physical prostration we felt a certain energy; instead of annihilation in the Presence of God, we felt exultation and joy. Instead of any difficulty in speaking, we felt an enthusiasm in communicating what we had seen and heard, though indeed, we felt a strong inspiration to keep some things secret."

Our space does not allow of our entering more fully into the story of the beautiful lives of these dear little peasant children of Fatima, so highly honored by God's Holy Mother. We merely wish to accentuate one fact and that is the amazing results produced in them by the Angel's visits.

No master of the spiritual life could instill into their minds such lofty ideals, such heroic courage, such unbounded generosity in doing God's will. Let this be a lesson to us, for if we are devoted to our own dear Angel Guardian, he too will most certainly raise us up to a great height of sanctity and obtain for us the very greatest graces.

WHY DID THE ANGEL APPEAR IN PORTUGAL?

Although every country, every kingdom, and every province has its Angel Guardian, we know of no other nation in *modern* times whose Angel has appeared as in [the case of] Portugal. Can we offer any explanation for this exceptional honor? Perhaps the answer lies in the fact that Portugal has had from the earliest times a very special love for the Angels, as the following facts go to show:

Her first king, Don Afonso Henriques, a man eminent not only for his military prowess but also for his truly Christian life, had a very marked love for the Angels, notably for his Angel Guardian and for St. Michael, the prince of the heavenly host.

We find this devotion mentioned in some of the old Portuguese chronicles. The account runs as follows:

Some time after the king had taken the almost impregnable Moorish fortress of Santarem, the Moorish hosts, under the command of their monarch Albaraque, in person, made a formidable attack on the city in the hope of reconquering it. At the time king Afonso Henriques was suffering grievously from a wound in one of his legs so that he could not mount his horse. He insisted, however, on getting into a chariot and joining in the fight. It was a hazardous adventure because his death or capture would have been a serious blow to his soldiers and a source of encouragement to his enemies.

However, as events proved, he was under angelic protection. A legend says he saw an arm grasping a sword and also a wing, which showed him that an Angel was with him.

This sword protected the person of the king and wrought dreadful havoc among the Moors, who fled in terror, leaving the Portuguese masters of the field. The Moorish captives taken in the battle declared that they too had seen the Angel.

In gratitude the king founded a military Order which he called the "Order of the Wing" in honor of St. Michael and the Angels.

Many noble families belonged to this Order, and we have seen an image of a wing and an arm brandishing a sword, on the coat of arms of one of the old families.

We have further evidence of this devotion in the fact that Don Manuel I, one of the most remarkable of the Kings of Portugal, was also most devoted to the Angels, so much so that he begged the Pope to sanction the feast of the Angel Guardian of Portugal and permit the Office and Mass to be said on the third Sunday of July. This feast is still celebrated. We have never heard that any other country celebrates a like feast.

Vasco da Gama, the renowned discoverer who found the maritime route to India, leaves another proof of the great confidence that the Portuguese had in the holy Angels.

When starting on this memorable voyage to India, one of the most remarkable recorded in history, he called two of his ships after the Angels, one *St. Gabriel,* because it was he who had brought to the world the great tidings of our Redemption—and the Admiral too, had the wish to carry the same news of salvation to the pagan lands he hoped to discover. He called the other ship *St. Raphael,* after the Angel who accompanied the young Tobias on his long and dangerous journey. The Admiral rightly thought that he himself could have no better guide and protector on this perilous voyage than this patron of travellers.

In modern times the Portuguese, recalling this act of Vasco da Gama, have again named two of their vessels after the Archangels.

The King Cardinal Don Henrique cherished a marked love for the Angels and built a Church in their honor in Lisbon. The feast day was kept as a Holiday of Obligation in the parish. A second church was erected in honor of St. Michael, and his feast was also observed as a Holiday of Obligation.

In other churches of Lisbon and throughout the country we find still further traces of this same devotion.

Many of the Kings of Portugal and also the royal princes took the names of Michael, Gabriel, and Raphael in Baptism.

In some families the name of one of the Angels is given as a second name to all the children. In one such family known to the writer, there was John Raphael, Mary Raphael, Thomas Raphael, James Raphael and Anne Raphael.

Luiz de Sousa, O.P., one of the foremost Portuguese writers, gives us the story of the conversion of the celebrated Frei Gil or Egidius of Santarem, by his Angel Guardian.

Egidius was a man of noble birth and of a devout Christian family. He himself, unfortunately, took to the study of the black arts and went to Paris in order *to facilitate this study.* On his way he was induced to sell his soul to the devil in exchange for great learning. This he did by a written bond. One night when working in his laboratory, a young man mounted on a horse dashed into the chamber and sternly rebuking him ordered him to desist at once from his diabolical practices. Egidius was terrified and at once obeyed. Some time after he was again tempted by the devil, who persuaded him that this vision was merely the effect of an overheated imagination, and he resumed his studies.

The horseman once more appeared and, standing over him, struck him with his lance, leaving a mark on his chest, and in a voice of anger, such as he had never heard before, commanded him to renounce these *hellish arts* at once and forever.

Egidius, moved by this second apparition to the very depths of his soul, not only abandoned his evil ways but did salutary penance.

He returned to Portugal, where he joined the Dominican Order, in which he attained great sanctity.

The same chronicler cites another example of angelic visitation. One of the Fathers, eminent for holiness, by name Father Lawrence, was accosted one day, when making a journey on foot, by an Angel who presented him with a box of relics which he had brought from a distant town recently taken by the Saracens and which he wished to save from desecration. These relics were for many centuries venerated in the Church of Guimarães in the north of Portugal.

These few incidents go to show how deeply ingrained was the love and devotion to the holy Angels in Portugal. They furnish us with a possible reason why the Guardian Angel of the country appeared in Fatima, for the Angels generously repay all the honor we show them.

ANGELIC APPARITIONS IN HUNGARY AND IN IRELAND

As we have already observed, we know of no other country except Portugal where the Angel Guardian of the country has appeared in recent times, but the Angels have appeared in remoter epochs in Hungary and in Ireland, both of which countries have also been very devoted to the Angels.

Olibrio, King of Hungary. This king was deliberating on making war on the Tartars, trusting to a powerful army which he had at his disposal. A holy Bishop counselled him to pray fervently before deciding on hostilities. In answer to his sincere prayer, the Angel Guardian of the Kingdom appeared and warned him not to declare the war he had meditated on making, for said the Angel, "Your cause is not just and you will surely be defeated. Do not trust in your army, for the Angel Guardian of the Tartars will fight against you, and you will be beaten, and I cannot help you in what is not just."

The King very readily followed this advice and made peace with the Tartars, who gladly accepted his overtures, for in this his Angel helped him.

In deep gratitude the monarch celebrated magnificent festivities in honor of the Angel Guardian of the Kingdom and placed an image of the Angel over his crown.

Thenceforward it became the custom of the Kings of Hungary to ask God's help in all matters of moment through the intercession of the Angel Guardian of the Kingdom.

The King of Ireland and the Angel. The Venerable Bede mentions that one of the Kings of Ireland had great devotion to the Holy Angels and invoked them frequently with the greatest confidence.

Unfortunately, owing to the bad advice of a false counsellor, he became unpopular with his subjects who determined to revolt against him.

On learning this, the King was seriously disturbed and entertained grave fears for his life and kingdom. However his Angel Guardian appeared to him radiant with joy and bade him not to fear, for he said, "Owing to your great love for me and the other Angels, we have obtained from God that your princes and subjects will remain loyal and faithful to you. But do you, on your part, dismiss your false counsellor and seek in all things to please our people."

The King gratefully did what the Angel had counselled him, with the happiest results.

These two incidents teach us how our Angels, though they love us dearly, will not help us if we seek to do wrong. On the other hand, they are eager to give us every possible assistance when we seek for what is just. We should beware of speaking ill or doing harm to others, for their Angels will defend them and avenge them.

Our Lord seems to call our attention to this fact when He warns us not to harm or scandalize children, for He says, "Their Angels see the face of My Father."

St. Columba and the Angels. St. Columba, Abbot of Iona, was one of the greatest of the Irish Saints. He cherished a great love for the Angels who constantly visited him. Before his birth an Angel told his mother that she would bring forth a son who would take numberless souls to Heaven and who would be reckoned amongst the Prophets.

He was once falsely accused of a crime he had never committed. He boldly went to the synod convoked to condemn and punish him. When the great St. Brendan, who was present, saw him approach, he went to meet him, showing him every sign of reverence. The other members of the synod were surprised.

He replied, I saw a brilliant pillar of fire precede this man whom you have unjustly excommunicated, and I have seen Angels walking by his side.

When living in the Isle of Hindba, an Angel came three successive times to bid him consecrate Aeden King.

He saw the soul of Brito the monk, then the soul of a holy man called Diarmid, and later on, the soul of St. Brendan borne up to Heaven by Angels.

The demons, furious at the good he did, attacked him fiercely, but he expelled them from the Island.

When praying in his cell, he suddenly called out: "Help, help," for he had seen a monk fall from a high tower. The Angel seized the falling monk before he reached the ground and so saved his life.

He sought out lonely places in the woods to pray where bands of Angels surrounded him. When he died, his soul mounted to Heaven with innumerable Angels.

Chapter 2

SOME ANGELIC APPEARANCES IN OUR OWN DAYS

We shall now mention briefly some other angelic apparitions made to eminent servants of God in our own days. Our information is culled from various reliable sources.

SAINT GEMMA GALGANI

This dear little Saint was born in 1878, died in 1903 and was canonized in 1940. She was favored, not at one time or other, but we might say *constantly,* by the visible presence of her Angel Guardian, whose radiant beauty and sweet goodness filled her with delight. She conversed lovingly with him, while he on his part gave her proofs daily of his tender love and friendship. He was with her everywhere, at prayer, at work in her room, when performing household duties and even in the streets.

This constant presence of her Angel and his intimate communication with her were no illusion. Her confessor, who was an experienced master of the spiritual life, used all the means counselled by the Church to make sure of the genuineness of these visions and apparitions.

Her interviews with the dear Angel were of a simple and familiar nature. She chatted with him, gazed on his face, asked him many questions, to which he replied with ineffable love and affection.

He took messages from her to Our Lord, to the Blessed Virgin and the Saints and brought her back their answers. Moreover this glorious Angel took the tenderest care of his protegée. He taught her how to pray and meditate, especially on the Passion and sufferings of Our Lord. He gave her admirable counsels and lovingly reproved her when she committed any little faults. Under his guidance, Gemma speedily reached a high degree of perfection.

Once when a wicked man uttered a horrible blasphemy in her hearing, the little Saint was so horrified that she would have fallen to the ground had not the Angel grasped her by the hand and consoled her by a few loving words.

On another occasion, when she had delayed overlong at her devotions in the church, he accompanied her home.

When sick and suffering, as she frequently was, her Angel ever watched by her side with unceasing care so that she said to one of her friends, "How could I have ever borne those awful pains had it not been for the presence of my Angel?"

These are some of the countless beautiful incidents which her biographers relate at great length and with many interesting details regarding the delightfully familiar intercourse which existed for many years between this pious maiden and her Angel Guardian.

This dear child was not only privileged to see and speak with her Angel, but our dear Lord and His Blessed Mother appeared to her also and treated her with the gentlest love and affection. In order to merit these wonderful privileges, her Angel sought to make her humble, pure and full of divine love.

We may not aspire perhaps to such visible communications with our own Angel Guardian, but yet Gemma Galgani teaches us a lesson of the very highest importance, *viz.*, that we have an Angel as really and truly present with us as she had, though we do not see him. This dear Angel loves us, just as her Angel loved her, with an immense love and is as able and as ready to help us as her Angel helped her.

We would do well to ask this little Saint to obtain for us the grace to feel and realize that our Angel is with us. It does not matter whether we see him or not. The great thing is to know and *feel* that he is certainly with us and never leaves us.

(For further information, our readers should read what the Saint's confessor has written about her.)

SAINT JOHN BOSCO

Was it an Angel or was it a dog? The life of Don Bosco furnishes us with a remarkable and interesting story of what appears to many an angelic intervention in saving the life of this servant of God from the fierce attacks of the Waldensian heretics, who made several attempts to assassinate him.

These heretics were furious at the good done by Don Bosco and sought by violent means to rid themselves of his influence. Some of their adherents were men of the lowest and most vicious type, and these they hired to carry out their nefarious designs.

When returning home one night through a bad and dangerous part of the town, he saw a magnificent dog of huge size following him. At first he was frightened but quickly came to see that the dog was friendly. The animal walked by his side and accompanied him to the door of his house and then went away. This happened five, six or eight times. He called the dog Grigio.

What did it mean? He was soon to learn.

Hastening home by himself, some time after the first appearance of the dog, two shots were fired at him by an assassin from behind a tree. Both shots missed their mark, but his assailant then rushed at and grappled with him. At that moment, Grigio appeared and sank his teeth into the flesh of the would-be murderer, who fled away shrieking with pain.

On a second occasion, two men lay in wait for him and threw a sack over his head. This time it seemed all was over with him, but Grigio unexpectedly came to his rescue and jumped at one of the ruffians, seizing him by the throat. The

other fled in terror. Don Bosco had then to liber-
ate the first from the fangs of Grigio, who still
held him by the throat.

A third time, no less than twelve hired assas-
sins, armed with clubs, lay in ambush, into which
Don Bosco walked unawares. Again, escape
seemed impossible, but once more Grigio
bounded into the midst of the group, and his
fierce look and savage growl proved enough. The
men made off as quickly as they could.

Sometimes the dog entered Don Bosco's house,
but always with some reason, either to accompany
him on a night journey or to prevent his leaving
the house. No amount of animal instinct could
explain these unexpected appearances of the dog.

On one of these occasions, when Don Bosco
tried to go out, the great dog lay across the door
and growled in such a menacing way that St. John
was forced to remain at home. And it was well
that he did so, for shortly afterwards a gentleman arrived to warn him not to leave the house
on any consideration, as the heretics lay in wait
to kill him.

As long as the persecution lasted, Grigio never
failed to be at his post and when the danger
passed he was seen no more. Whence he came
or whither he went no one knew.

Ten years later, Don Bosco had to go to the
farmhouse of some friends and had been advised
that the road was dangerous.

"If only I had Grigio," he said. At once the great
dog appeared by his side, as if he had heard the

words, giving signs of the greatest joy. Both man and dog arrived safely at the farmhouse and went into the dining room, where the family invited Don Bosco to take part in the evening meal.

The dog lay down. No one thought any more of him. When the repast was finished the master of the house proposed to feed the dog. But he was gone! Doors and windows had been closed; how did he go?

In 1883, that was more than thirty years after the dog's first appearance, he appeared once more in a different locality to guide Don Bosco, who had lost his way.

How [are we to] explain those wonderful appearances of the dog, at the most opportune moments and in different localities? Surely we may believe that this was angelic intervention. [Especially is this so because the great dog was never known to eat.]

PERE LAMY
(1853-1931)

Père Lamy was of our own days. He was indeed a most beautiful and lovable character, raised by God to a great height of sanctity and favored by the most extraordinary graces.

He reminds us strikingly of the Curé of Ars, so simple, so humble and yet so powerful in work, so enlightened by the Holy Spirit.

The facts we quote here are guaranteed by competent authorities, who when writing or speaking of him, give these facts as far as possible in Père Lamy's own words.

Although he was the recipient of many wonderful graces and privileges, we confine ourselves here to an account of his intimacy with the Angels.

These blessed Spirits are attracted to us particularly by the virtues of purity, humility, sobriety and love, all of which virtues shone brightly in the life of Père Lamy.

The highest authorities, such as Cardinal Amette, bore witness to the good Father's amazing sanctity. His Eminence did not hesitate to say of him, "In my diocese I have a second Curé of Ars."

Some of his friends actually heard the Angels speaking to him. The following is a fact given us by his personal and very intimate friend, Count Biver, who wrote his life:

"On November 19th, 1924, at a quarter-past ten, I was in bed in Fr. Lamy's house. I had put out my light. Two or three minutes had passed when, through the two doors which are rather thin, I heard an animated conversation going on in the priest's room. There were three voices taking part in it, and in the silence of the night they could be distinguished clearly and distinctly. I was at once intensely interested in this phenomenon, the importance of which I grasped immediately. Despite the cold, I sat up in order to hear better. Nobody had come upstairs since I had entered my bedroom. The stairs are so light and the house so far from being soundproof, that from my room

I could have heard the slightest movements. Only twenty minutes earlier, when I left the priest at the door of his room, I had seen that there was no other occupant.

"From time to time Père Lamy spoke definitely and affirmatively. I could distinguish a little here and there, but did not understand all the words and meaning of what was said. Discretion forbade me to get out of bed and listen at the door.

"On the following morning, at a quarter to six, I rejoined Père Lamy as he was going downstairs. On the way to the church, I put the question to him: 'Father, after bidding me goodnight last evening, you were talking. I heard other voices too. . .Were they Angels?' He smiled and answered, 'Perhaps! They are the evening's consolation.'

"In answer to further questions which I put to him during that day, my host told me that the voices I had heard were those of St. Gabriel and his Guardian Angel.

"He said, 'We do not give the Angels the importance they deserve; we do not pray to them enough. The Angels are very much touched when we pray to them. It is very useful to pray to the Angels.

"'We do not pray enough to our Guardian Angels. What do we do for them? We give them just a bit of a prayer at the end of our night prayers; that's all. Their mercy in our regard is very great, and often we do not make sufficient use of them. They regard us as brothers in need, and they are very good to us.

"'There is nobody so faithful as an Angel. What a memory he has! He remembers everything. He can tell you what you did ten years ago as if it were only yesterday. What a number of friends we have whom we do not know! We are very little in comparison with them.' And thus he chatted very simply about the Angels.

"'Our Guardian Angels often save us from accidents. But what can they do for us when we are not in the state of grace? They would like to help us, but they cannot. When we refuse homage to Our Lord, we send His servants away. And how many of us Christians ever ask for their aid and their protection? A little prayer: "Goodnight, my good Angel," and that is all! We do not have recourse enough to the Angels. They are with us and we leave them alone. We don't trouble them as much as we ought to.

"'Their garments are white, but with an unearthly whiteness. I cannot describe it, because it cannot be compared to earthly whiteness; it is much softer to the eye. These bright Angels are enveloped in a light so different from ours that in comparison everything seems dark. When you see a band of fifty, you are lost in amazement. They seem clothed with golden plates, constantly moving, and are like so many suns. It must be a wonderful sight in Heaven to see millions of Angels.

"'I have often been supported by Angels when I was tired and exhausted and carried from one place to another without knowing it. I would merely say, "God, I am tired."

"'Often at night, I would be far away from home, and I would find myself suddenly transported almost to my door.

"'I used to go to the railway station during the war and give general absolution to the soldiers. It was in the evening at the station. There were about two hundred soldiers lying on stretchers or planks, and even one on the ground. Cars were coming from Paris to pick them up. When I arrived, I always asked my Guardian Angel to cure some of them. I saw the Angel and the Archangel blessing them, and I passed on. The Archangel St. Gabriel was with me, and so was my Guardian Angel. While he was there, I could see quite clearly. He illuminated men's consciences so that you could see.

"'Cardinal Amette had said to me, "I grant you full faculties, my dear Father. I know that you will not do anything wrong." In the midst of so much sorrow and distress, I had the consolation of seeing that the Archangel was very merciful to the soldiers.

"'The Angels saved me from being stung by bees in the chapel. It was last summer. As I could not see very well I should have suffered tortures. They forbade the bees to sting me.'"

These are a few of the many facts which were crowded into the life of this dear old priest.

It is for us to bear clearly in mind what he tells us, namely, that we do not give anything like the love and trust we ought to give to our own dear Angel and to the Angels in general.

(Count Biver's life of Père Lamy, though very simple in style, is interesting and instructive. A translation in English may be obtained from TAN Books and Publishers, Inc.)

THE STORY OF TUNDALE

Tundale was an Irish knight, a brave man, a good soldier, but unfortunately he led a bad life. The following story of his conversion made such an impression that it was translated into German, French, Italian, English, Norman, Norse and Irish. It was written by an Irish monk about the year 1149.

Once, when sitting at table, Tundale became unconscious and would have been buried had not his body retained some little warmth. He remained in this unconscious state from Wednesday to Saturday.

On regaining consciousness, he was completely changed, gave thanks to God and did severe penance for his bad life. He told his friends that his soul seemed to have left his body and he found himself surrounded by demons, who strove to take him to Hell, but his Angel Guardian appeared and drove them away. Tundale told the Angel how grievously he suffered and the Angel in reply said: I have been always by your side but you never asked me to help you. He promised Tundale that he should receive mercy but would suffer for some time. Then, led by the Angel, he passed through Hell, Purgatory and Heaven, suffering at first, but then comforted. He saw people whom he had known on Earth. He saw St. Patrick and other Irish Saints in Heaven, and he saw two Irish Kings in Purgatory.

These facts made a deep impression on all who heard them and were translated, as we said above, into many languages.

Chapter 3

ALL ABOUT THE ANGELS

WHO ARE THE ANGELS?

The Angels are pure spirits, the mighty Princes of Heaven who stand before God, gazing on His unveiled presence. They are burning fires of love, filled to overflowing with the plenitude of happiness.

The Angels are the perfect images of God, mirrors of His Divine perfections, reflecting His love, His beauty, His Holiness, His Power, all His Divine attributes and perfections, but each Angel in his own special way.

No two Angels are alike, no two are equal. God's perfections are infinite, and the countless millions of Angels reflect these perfections in a divinely marvelous way. No two men, no two women, are identically alike, but the difference between them is relatively slight, whereas the difference between two Angels is vast, complete. Every Angel is specifically different from the other as one species differs from another. All the millions of men and women who people the world, all those who have ever lived or ever will live are of one and the same species, but each Angel is a species all in himself!

The Angels are unspeakably lovely, they have no shadow of imperfection, no defects. Nothing on this earth can possibly give us an idea of their resplendent glory. No painter, no poet, no artist ever conceived anything like them. They are living replicas of God's beauty.

Fra Angelico's pictures of the Angels excel those of any other artist so that Michelangelo exclaimed on seeing them: "Angelico must have seen these Angels in Heaven; otherwise, he could never have painted them as he has done." But even Angelico's pictures do not give us the faintest idea of the real Angels.

St. Bridget, who was favored by God with heavenly visions, tells us that were we to see an Angel in all his beauty, we should be so ravished with delight at the sight of him that we should die of love.

St. Frances of Rome was favored by the constant vision of her Angel. She says that were an Angel to appear in all his splendor, the light of the sun and moon and stars would become dim in comparison.

After Our Lord's Resurrection, we read how an Angel descended from Heaven and rolled back the stone that had closed the holy sepulchre. The Sacred Scriptures say that the countenance of the Angel was like lightning and his raiment white as snow. His appearance was so full of majesty that the soldiers whom Christ's enemies had placed to guard the tomb were terrified and dared not to look on him, but fell to the ground as if dead.

When, therefore, the Angels appear to men, they take a human form so as not to over-awe or confound those who look on them.

What must be the ravishing beauty of the Heavenly Jerusalem, where these countless millions of glorious Angels are not only resplendently beautiful but all differ from each other so that the perfections of one are completely different from those of the other.

The Angels reflect God's goodness and sweetness no less wonderfully. They reflect all His divine virtues and perfections, they enjoy the vision of God's infinite love, and they love Him back with all the mighty strength and intensity of their natures.

Their happiness is perfect, for they receive of *the ocean of God's happiness* in a way that no human mind can fathom. The happiness that an Angel enjoys in one moment is so deep, complete and all-satisfying that it exceeds all the happiness that a mortal man could enjoy in a thousand years.

THE GENEROSITY OF THE ANGELS

What is of paramount importance to us is that the Holy Angels seek in every possible way to share with us this immense ocean of love and happiness which they themselves enjoy. Their generosity knows no bounds.

This is a truth that we must do our best to understand fully and clearly. Were a very rich man to say to us, "Ask me for everything you wish and

I will most readily give it to you," how happy we should be! Certainly we would not hesitate to ask for all we need.

This is exactly what the Angels say to us: "Ask us and we will give you a share of all our treasures, all our graces, all our happiness, and we will give you some of all we have." Their goodness and generosity are immense.

Unfortunately, so far from corresponding with their efforts for our welfare, we constantly *impede* them by our sins and imperfections. If only we knew them better and loved them more, and were more docile to their constant whisperings, our happiness would be unspeakably great.

WHAT ARE THE ANGELS DOING?

Millions and millions of Angels fill the Heavens, ministering unto God, but millions and millions of Angels are also here on Earth, ministering unto us. They are in our midst, around us, about us, everywhere.

Their activity in our regard is unceasing every day and every moment of the day, though we do not see them nor even suspect their presence nor feel their influence. They are watching over us with infinite care and love.

Were it not for their ever-vigilant protection, the history of the world would be far different, far more calamitous than it has been.

The life too, of each of us, had we not a mighty Angel guarding us, would be sad in the extreme.

What the life of a little child would be if abandoned, forsaken, without mother, father, or friend, such would be in great part our lot had not God, in His mercy, given us our holy Angel.

These Angels are helping us at every instant, doing us countless favors and saving us from dangers and evils of every kind. God has given us into their charge: "For he hath given his angels charge over thee; to keep thee in all thy ways. In their hands they shall bear thee up: lest thou dash thy foot against a stone." (*Ps.* 90:11-12).

ANGELIC INTELLIGENCE

The Angels, like God, have two great faculties: the Intellect and the Will. The intellect of the Angel is incomparably superior to the human intellect. The Angels are not only perfect in beauty, mighty in strength, but they are full of knowledge and wisdom.

Their manner of understanding is likewise completely different from ours. The human mind has to plod from truth to truth just as the human body moves step by step, whereas the angelic intelligence grasps the whole of a subject at a single glance. Seeing a principle, it sees at once all its consequences, seeing a truth it sees at the same time all its possible aspects.

The most notable savants of this Earth have amassed the knowledge of a limited number of subjects with infinite labor and long years of study. Nor may they claim the credit for all they know for they began where others had left off, and others will continue from where they have left off. The knowledge, too, thus acquired at the cost of such labor is frequently mingled with errors, mistakes and doubts, whereas the knowledge of the Angels is clear, certain and free from all possibility of error.

ST. ALBERT THE GREAT

One of the greatest scholars that the world has ever seen, especially of the natural sciences, was St. Albert the Great. Wimmer says of him that "he explained the whole universe from the stones on the ground to the stars in the heavens." He wrote with amazing lucidity and completeness on astronomy, meteorology, physics, mechanics, chemistry, mineralogy, anthropology, zoology and botany. He has described minutely the life and manners of ants, bees, spiders and other insects. His works also deal with vegetable life—plants and trees. He has treated with great authority on earthquakes, volcanoes, the ebb and flow of the tides, the secrets of the ocean and various other subjects.

In philosophy he is accounted by some as greater than St. Thomas, though he is inferior to him in theology. His grasp of the sacred sciences was on a par with his knowledge of the natural sciences.

Now that seven centuries have passed since he taught in the schools, the scholars of today are amazed at the vastness and accuracy of his work.

Yet the intellect of this prodigy of science bears no comparison with the intellect of the Angels, and his amazing knowledge is little when compared to that of these blessed spirits.

For the Angels know all the secrets of nature; they see into the center of the Earth, into the depths of the sea; they have all natural knowledge. They know more about health and medicine than all the doctors in the world, more about the stars and the heavens than all the astronomers who ever lived or ever will live. All sciences are known to them in their most absolute perfection, besides which, God fills their intelligence with very oceans of supernatural light.

THE POWER OF THE ANGELS

The second great faculty of the Angels is the will, and this, too, is incomparably superior to the human will.

When an Angel wills, he never draws back. He wills with all his possible power, and there can be no change. His decisions are certain and irrevocable, for they are made with all necessary information about what he wills. In what he does there is no struggle, no conflict; he bears down opposition with irresistible might. In this again he is an image of God's strength.

We have some examples of angelic power in the Sacred Scriptures.

The Egyptians, as we read in *Genesis,* held God's Chosen People in cruel bondage. God, to punish

the oppressors and deliver His people, sent an
Angel who slew 70,000 Egyptians in one night!

On another occasion, Sennacherib, the
Emperor of Assyria, sent up a mighty army against
Jerusalem and demanded its surrender, mocking
at the same time and insulting the God of Israel.
The Almighty sent His Angel, who slew 185,000
Assyrians in a single night.

The Angels could have as well slain millions
of men as these few thousands.

THE ANGELS GUIDE THE STARS, THE MOON, THE SUN AND THE PLANETS

St. Thomas, incidentally, gives us another proof
of the angelic strength. He teaches that each great
star, planet, sun, and every heavenly body, even
the greatest, has each a Guardian Angel who keeps
it in its course and prevents any possible aberra-
tion. What prodigious energy and power does not
such control demand!

It is true that all the stars and heavenly bodies,
by the natural direction given them by God, pur-
sue their several courses, but these great worlds
are material and therefore, as the Angelic Doctor points out, are liable to decay and deteriora-
tion. To prevent, therefore, disorder and confusion
in the thousands of heavenly bodies which are
whirling through space with inexpressible speed,
God gives each one, in His all-wise Providence,
an Angel to keep it in its course and avert the
dire calamities that would result were it to stray

from its allotted orbit.

Few people think of all this when, on beautiful star-lit nights, they gaze on the Heavens and the myriads of stars. How fitting it would be to salute the countless Angels who guard these stars: "O, glorious Angels of the stars, we love you, we thank you! Please bless us and shower on us your graces."

CARDINAL NEWMAN FOLLOWS ST. THOMAS

The subject of angelic operations in the powers of nature has been beautifully illustrated by Cardinal Newman in one of his Parochial Sermons:

"What a number of beautiful and wonderful objects does Nature present on every side to us! and how little do we know concerning them! In some, indeed, we see symptoms of intelligence, and we get to form some idea of what they are. For instance, about brute animals we know little, but still we see they have sense and we understand that their bodily form, which meets the eye, is but the index, the outside token, of something we do not see...But why do rivers flow? Why does rain fall? Why does the sun warm us? and the wind, why does it blow? Here our natural reason is at fault...Reason tells us of no spirit abiding in what is commonly called the *things* of the world, to make them perform their ordinary duties. Of course, it is God's will which sustains all; so does God's will enable us to move also, yet this does not hinder, but, in one sense, we may be truly said to move ourselves; but how do

the wind and water, earth and fire move? Now
here Scripture interposes, and seems to tell us
that all this wonderful harmony is the work of
Angels.

"Those events which we ascribe to chance, as
the weather, or to nature, as the seasons, are duties
done to that God who maketh His Angels to be
winds, and His Ministers a flame of fire. For example, it was an Angel which gave to the pool
at Bethsaida its medicinal quality, and there is
no reason why we should doubt that other health-
springs in this and other countries are made such
by a like, though unseen ministry. The fires on
Mount Sinai, the thunders and lightnings, were
the work of Angels; and in the *Apocalypse* we read
of the Angels restraining the winds. Works of
vengeance are likewise attributed to them. The
fiery law of the volcanoes, which (as it appears)
was the cause of Sodom and Gomorrah's ruin,
was brought about by the two Angels who res-
cued Lot. The pestilence in Israel, when David
numbered the people, was the work of an Angel.
The earthquake at the Resurrection was the work
of an Angel.

"And in other parts of the *Apocalypse* we read
how the earth was smitten in various ways by
Angels of vengeance.

"Thus, as far as the Scripture communications
go, we learn that the course of Nature, which is
so wonderful, so beautiful, and at times, so fearful, is effected by the ministry of these unseen
beings. Nature is not inanimate, its daily toil is

intelligent; its works are duties. As our souls move our bodies, be our bodies what they may, so there are Spiritual intelligences which move those wonderful and vast portions of the natural world which seem to be inanimate; and as the gestures, speech, and expressive countenances of our friends around help us to hold intercourse with them, so in the motions of universal Nature, in the interchange of day and night, Summer and Winter, wind and storm, fulfilling His word, we are reminded of the blessed and dutiful Angels.

"Whenever we look abroad, we are reminded of those most gracious and holy Beings, the servants of the Holiest, who deign to minister to the heirs of salvation. Every breath of air, and ray of light and heat, every beautiful prospect are, as it were, the skirts of their garments, the waving of the robes of those whose faces see God in Heaven."

It is indeed sad that so many people ignore these glorious Angels. Let us, Dear Readers, for the future recognize these gracious spirits, our elder brothers, our dearest friends. Let us speak to them, enjoy their company, ask them lovingly for all we need. No mother on Earth gives as readily to her children what the Angels are eager to give to us.

HOW DO THE ANGELS MOVE?

The movement of the Angels is marvelous. In a single instant, an Angel comes from Heaven to Earth or goes from one end of the universe to the other without passing through the intermediate space. To understand this angelic movement, we have only to compare it with our thought. In a moment our thought passes from Heaven to Earth, from England to China, from end to end of the Earth. Angels are, if we might say so, living thoughts, and they move even as our thought.

Light travels at the speed of 225,000 miles a second. Light comes from the sun to our Earth at the same rate and takes 8 minutes and 15 seconds to arrive, but the movement of the *Angels* is unspeakably more rapid—they come in one instant.

Another notable fact about these glorious spirits is that they can be in two or more places at the same time, even though these places be thousands of miles distant. They are in no way subject to the laws of space.

Though ever with us and devoting all their care and attention to our welfare, they never lose sight of the presence of God. They are always gazing on His infinite beauty, basking in the sunshine of His Presence.

ARE THE ANGELS MORE NUMEROUS THAN MEN?

The number of the Angels exceeds all our power of calculation or conception. If we think of the number of the stars in the heavens, of the number of leaves on the trees, of all the forests in the world, of the innumerable grains of sand on all the seashores, of the drops of water in the ocean, of all the men who ever lived, all material things put together would not give us the smallest idea of the number of the Angels.

There are three great hierarchies of Angels and in each hierarchy there are three choirs, that is, nine choirs in all.

They are thus divided: the Seraphs, the Cherubs and the Thrones form the hierarchy which stands nearest the Throne of God.

Then the Dominations, Virtues and Powers form the second hierarchy.

The Principalities, Archangels and Angels are the third order.

The higher the choir, the more numerous are its Angels, so that the Seraphs, in number, far exceed all the others.

WHERE DO WE GET OUR KNOWLEDGE OF THE ANGELS?

The **first** great fount of information about the Angels is Sacred Scripture, the inspired Word of God. Both the Old and the New Testaments tell us many and beautiful things about the great Princes of Heaven.

Secondly, Christ's infallible Church teaches the most consoling doctrines about the Angels.

Thirdly, Tradition has handed down to us from the earliest days important truths regarding the Angels.

Fourthly, the unanimous teaching of the Doctors and Saints throws floods of light on this doctrine.

Fifthly, our reason recognizes not only the possibility of the existence of Angels but the fitness, the necessity of their existence, for otherwise there would be a great gap so to speak in the harmonious arrangement in the plan of creation, which is so divinely perfect.

Pagan philosophers have recognized the existence of the Angels, and missionaries from far off pagan lands tell us that even the natives believe in the Spirit world.

Sixthly, we have innumerable well-authenticated accounts of apparitions of Angels — indisputable facts!

Chapter 4

WHERE ARE THE ANGELS?

This is a vastly important question and deserves our best attention.

The Angels are everywhere. Millions of them ever stand before God; millions of them, too, minister to us on earth, as we have already seen. They have charge not only of us but of all material things, of the sun, the moon, the stars, the planets, oceans, rivers, kingdoms, provinces. But what interests us most is that *each* man, *each* woman, *each* child, pagan or Christian, baptized or unbaptized, has an Angel all to himself or herself.

When we gather in a church, there are as many Angels truly present as there are men and women. When walking in the busy streets every day, we pass hundreds and thousands of glorious Angels. When we enter a hall, a tram-car, a train, we are in the midst of Angels. All the men and women whom we meet, whether young or old, rich or poor, saints or sinners, each one has his or her Angel, and since all these gracious spirits are living, vital intelligences and see and love us, we should do well to salute them. They will recognize our salutation and return it; they will appreciate our attention and repay us lovingly. Every enlightened Christian should make it his habit to treat these Angels reverently, yet familiarly and lovingly.

We do not salute the men or women we meet in the street or in the church or in trains. They would not perceive or recognize our salutation. Not so the Angels! They see us distinctly, they note our every gesture, they hear our message with the greatest joy and return it most generously. They will give us love for love, with the difference that they give us a thousand times more than we give them.

If some rare chance brings us into the presence of a King or Queen, we salute the royal personage and feel flattered if our salute is returned with a gracious smile, or with a few words, and still more if the royal person stops to speak with us.

We meet the Angels, not by chance, not seldom, but every day. They see us, they love us and repay every attention we show them with a substantial return. Yet so many make no account of them! What lamentable ignorance!

If we but say, "Dearest Angels here present, I honor and love you and give thanks to God for all the glory He has given you," every one of these hundreds of Angels will hear and receive with pleasure our greeting and will repay us with a special mark of friendship, for the Angels never do things by halves. They are not like us, poor mortals, they never forget and they never grow cold. When once they are our friends, they are our friends forever.

Fancy all the millions of dear, loving, watchful Angels in Africa, in China, in India, in Japan, in Protestant countries, too, in Norway, Sweden, Denmark, Germany, Scotland, England, North America, with their thousands of thousands of men and women who never think of their Angels, never say a prayer to them, never say one word of thanks for their tireless love, for the unceasing favors that these loving Angels are doing them. But what can we do?

We can offer our Masses, our Communions, our Rosaries from time to time to thank and to console these glorious Angels. They will return our love a thousandfold. How easy it is for us to make powerful friends.

DO THE ANGELS DESIRE OUR LOVE?

One may ask: "Do these great Angels really prize our poor love and friendship?" Most certainly. The great God Himself, the great Creator, the Lord of all the Angels, asks us for our love and gives us His infinite love in exchange. Nay, He promises us a special reward, an eternal reward for every little mark of friendship we show Him. One little act of love gives Him more pleasure than a thousand blasphemies give Him pain, as He has revealed to some of His chosen servants.

Mary most Holy, the beloved Queen of the Angels, longs too for our affection and most generously repays it.

It is not then surprising that the Holy Angels,

even the mighty Seraphs and Cherubs who stand around the throne of God and all the heavenly choirs, are exceedingly pleased when we show them some sign of love.

St. Gertrude tells us that one day she was inspired to offer her Holy Communion in honor of the nine choirs of Angels. God permitted her to see how radiantly happy and grateful they were for this act of love. She had never dreamed that she could give them such happiness.

We know that the Sacrifice of the Mass gives God infinite glory. It gives Him all the possible praise and love that He could desire. One Mass gives Him more honor than all creatures have ever given Him on Earth, or in Heaven.

If then we offer our Mass sometimes, at least once a week, in honor of the Angels, we give these blessed spirits the greatest possible joy.

We can also give them immense pleasure by offering our good works in their honor and thanking God for all the beauty and holiness and glory that He has given them. If we do so, they will repay us a thousand times over.

THE ANGELS IN THE CHURCHES

Above all, in the churches there are multitudes of Angels, loving, adoring God in raptures of delight. He is the same God whom they worship in Heaven. We should think of this when in church; it would be a source of great consolation to us. We should join our prayers with their prayers, for thus will God listen to our supplications with far greater mercy and love. Our prayers, frequently so cold, when joined with those of the Angels, become most efficacious.

THE ANGELS AND THE MASS

Multitudes of Angels assist at every Mass.

St. Gregory: "The Heavens open and the multitudes of Angels come to assist at the Holy Sacrifice."

St. Augustine: "The Angels surround and help the priest when he is celebrating Mass."

St. John Chrysostom: "When Mass is being celebrated, the Sanctuary is filled with countless Angels who adore the Divine Victim immolated on the altar."

The efficacy of the Mass is so wonderful, God's mercy and generosity are then so unlimited that there is no moment so propitious to ask for favors as when Jesus is born on the altar. What we then ask for we shall almost certainly receive, and what we do not obtain in the Mass we may scarcely hope to receive by all other prayers, penances or pilgrimages. The Angels know this full well and come in multitudes to adore God and make their petitions at this hour of mercy. What an example for us!

We read in the revelations of St. Bridget: "One day, when I was assisting at the Holy Sacrifice, I saw an immense number of Holy Angels descend and gather around the altar, contemplating the priest. They sang heavenly canticles that ravished my heart; Heaven itself seemed to be contemplating the great Sacrifice. And yet we poor blind and miserable creatures assist at the Mass with so little love, relish and respect!"

Oh, if God would open our eyes, what wonders should we not see!

When Blessed Henry Suso, the Holy Dominican, was saying Mass, Angels in visible form gathered round the altar, and some came near to him in raptures of love.

This is what takes place at every Mass, though we do not see it.

Do Catholics ever think of this amazing truth, *viz.*, that at Mass they are praying in the midst of thousands of God's Angels?

The Angel and the roses. A poor farmer was wont to attend daily Mass for many years of his life.

He was crossing the snow-covered fields one cold morning on his way to church when he thought he heard footsteps behind him, and turning, he saw his Angel Guardian bearing a basket full of beautiful roses, which exhaled a delicious perfume.

"See," said the Angel, "these roses represent each step you have taken on the way to Mass, and each rose also represents a glorious reward which awaits you in Heaven. But far, far greater are the merits which you have obtained from the Mass itself."

HOW TO HONOR THE ANGELS AT MASS

At the beginning of Mass, let us remember what the Saints tell us, that multitudes of Angels assist at the Holy Sacrifice.

We are in the midst of these Angels, who see us and note all our movements. They are eager to help us and offer our prayers to God if we are devout. But if we are negligent and distracted, they are offended.

What a joy it is for us to feel that we are in the blessed company of these great Angels!

At the Gloria in Excelsis, let us join our voices with those of the priest and the Angels. This is the glorious canticle that they sang on the first Christmas night when Jesus was born. At Mass Jesus is born again, and again the blessed Spirits join with the priest in singing this same canticle. It is a wonderful prayer of adoration and praise and love. We must attend to its every word.

At the Preface, we join our voices with the Seraphs and Cherubs and all the nine choirs of Angels who are singing with ineffable delight **"Sanctus, Sanctus, Sanctus,"** etc. Our Lord bade St. Gertrude to give most special attention to the Preface and join with the Angels in praising Him.

At the Elevation, the Angels fall down and adore God even as they adore Him in Heaven. He is the same God, Omnipotent, Infinite, Eternal. How cold we are! We can change this coldness and indifference into burning fervor if we will join our adoration with that of the Angels.

St. Teresa appeared to one of her religious after death and said to her: "You should adore God on the altar just as we adore Him in Heaven, for He is the same God."

At the Communion, when the priest holds the Sacred Host in his hand and gives it to the people, the Angels surround him, gazing in wrapt ecstasy on that Miracle of miracles, God entering with such love into the souls of His creatures. They gaze on God with unspeakable happiness, but God never enters into them, never unites Himself to them as He does to us in Communion. Could we see these adoring Angels as they stand around the priest, our Communions would not be so tepid and so cold.

Let us at least ask the Angels to help us to receive our God with burning love and fervor.

A venerable priest once told the author how deeply sorry he was that for many years he had thought little about the Angels, but since he began to know and love them better, he finds a new joy and devotion in saying Mass.

Chapter 5

WHEN AND WHERE
WERE THE ANGELS CREATED?

The Angels were created at the same time the world was created, but before man. They were created in the state of grace and in the empyrean Heaven, not in the Heaven of the Blessed Trinity, i.e., not in the presence of God.

Had they once seen God, they would never have ceased to see and love Him.

They were created, therefore, in another Heaven, and here they had to give a proof of their fidelity to God and so merit the beatific vision.

They, like us, have free wills and, like us, had to choose between good and evil. True, in the angelic nature itself, as St. Thomas teaches, there is no strife, as there is in our poor natures, between the spirit and the flesh. But before they were admitted to the Beatific Vision, they had to choose between their nature, already in the state of grace, and the still higher state of that grace which would admit them to the immediate presence of God forever.

No creature, however perfect, not even the Princes of the Angels, could see God without that most special grace which theologians call the *Light of glory*. Before being admitted to see God, they were tried.

In this trial, by far the greater number remained faithful to God and were immediately received into the Heaven of the Blessed Trinity and were allowed to gaze on the unveiled beauty of God. Once here, they could sin no more.

Some of these, the faithful Angels, always stand before God and are called the *assisting* Angels. These are the Seraphs, Cherubs and Thrones.

St. Thomas thinks that these never come to Earth.

Others, while always enjoying God's presence, minister to us and are called the ministering Angels. These are the Dominations, Virtues and Powers, who guard the greater things of the Universe; and the Principalities, Archangels, and Angels who give their care more especially to us.

Unfortunately, many of the Angels fell at the moment of trial—some think as many as a third of the Heavenly Host. They fell through the sin of pride, preferring their own will to that of God in the time of trial. At the moment of their fall, they were precipitated into Hell.

Their great natures, their intellects and wills retained their pristine strength and power, but their love and sanctity were transformed by their sin into implacable malice and hate.

Seeing that they cannot attack God, they *direct* their fierce vengeance and vent their spleen on us, who are destined to fill the thrones they have left vacant and enjoy the glory and happiness that they have forever forfeited.

These Angels fell, not all from one choir or other, but many fell from each choir. Some even of the highest and the holiest Angels were lost.

These are the demons of whom we shall speak later on.

WHO WILL FILL THE THRONES OF THE FALLEN ANGELS?

The thrones left vacant by the fall of these Angels will be given to those of us who remain faithful to God and merit Heaven.

The question thereby arises: "Who will fill the thrones of the Seraphs and Cherubs and other high Angels who fell? Can men pretend to such high places in Heaven?"

Yes, men also, men prepared by God with great graces and raised to the highest degree of sanctity will take the thrones even of the great Seraphs and Cherubs who have fallen. Though it is true that our natures are immeasurably lower than those of the mighty princes of Heaven, yet God raises us up by His Grace, which is a participation of His own Divine Nature, as St. Peter tells us, to be fully worthy of ranking even with the glorious Seraphs who stand around His Throne.

Holy Mary, God's dear Mother, Queen of Angels and Saints, is an example of this. She is holier and greater than all the Angels. She is on a plane all by herself, inferior to God but incomparably superior to all other creatures. Even at the first moment of her existence, she was greater and holier than the highest Angels.

St. Joseph, the Foster Father of Jesus and the most pure spouse of Mary, comes next.

Next, we may believe, rank the Apostles, Patriarchs and Prophets. Many, too, of the other great Saints, like St. Dominic, St. Francis, St. Ignatius, will, doubtless, fill glorious thrones near God.

We read in the story of the Blessed Jordan who succeeded St. Dominic as Master General of the Dominican Order that after his death God was pleased to manifest his sanctity in divers ways. He himself appeared to St. Lydwine and others, telling them of his special glory in Heaven, and saying that he ranked with the Prophets and Apostles.

St. Paul, too, the first hermit, who had dwelt in the desert from the age of sixteen until the age of 115, was also seen after death by St. Anthony, being carried to Heaven by the Angels and given a place among the Prophets and Apostles.

A pious author relates the legend of how once a holy man was shown in vision the glory of Heaven. He noted one high throne that was vacant and asked the Angel who accompanied him, "Whose throne is that?"

The Angel made answer. "That was the throne destined for Lucifer, but now Francis of Assisi will fill it. The mighty Lucifer fell through pride; the lowly Francis has been raised up by humility."

Chapter 6

OUR ANGEL GUARDIANS

We will now speak of what is for us the most interesting and important of all the facts concerning the Angels, namely, their *rôle* as our dearest, most intimate, most loving Guardians. Every Christian should strive to have a full comprehension of this doctrine and should realize vividly the presence of this Angel by his side.

WHEN DOES OUR ANGEL BEGIN TO TAKE CHARGE OF US?

The great St. Thomas tells us that the moment a child is born God calls one of His glorious Spirits and gives the newborn babe into his special care. It is not when the soul is created and united to our bodies—which takes place before our birth, for then the child is still one with its mother and protected by the mother's Angel—but it is when we are born into the world that our Angel begins his care of us, even before Baptism.

Every man, whether pagan, heretic or Catholic has a Guardian Angel. Though one Angel would be powerful enough to take perfect care of a thousand souls, yet God in His infinite goodness has given to each one of us a special Angel, an Angel who is all our own, whose great duty henceforth will be to watch over us day and night, asleep or awake, alone or in the midst of company, in our homes, in the street, working or resting, everywhere, every moment of our lives, in joys and in troubles. He never abandons us for a single instant; he sees our every movement; he is ever at our sides.

EACH ONE HAS A SPECIAL ANGEL

It seems at first sight incredible that God gives each of us poor mortals a glorious Prince of Heaven to guide and guard us all the days of our life, who is with us night and day, who devotes all his time, all his care, all his unceasing vigilance to secure our happiness.

But in pure truth, it is only one of the many immense proofs of love which our dear Lord has given us.

What *personal* favors has not God Himself already done us. Did He not create us with His own hands, making us to His own image and likeness? Did He not raise us up to the highest possible destiny that He could give us, namely, to be with Him as His dear children forever in Heaven, seated on thrones in His presence, enjoying infinite joys, the most perfect happiness for all eternity? Is He not our Father?

Did He not suffer and die for each one of us?

Does He not come into our souls, uniting Himself to us most intimately, countless times in Holy Communion? Does He not watch over us every moment so that not a single hair falls from our heads without His permission?

True, indeed, it is a wonderful proof of His love to give us a special Angel all to ourselves, to be our friend and protector, but it is only in keeping with what He has already done for us and it is to prepare us for what He still wishes to do for us.

But what is really amazing is that *we* do not appreciate, do not understand as we ought this divine favor; that we do not prize and love and seek to know better this glorious Angel who is so good to us. Our neglect of our dear Angel is appalling.

WHAT DOES OUR ANGEL DO FOR US?

We have already explained the great holiness, power and love of the Angels, how mighty their intellects are, how powerful their wills, and how irresistible their strength.

Now, when an Angel takes charge of a soul, he devotes all his glorious intelligence and knowledge, all his power and vigilance to protect, defend and help in every possible way the person whom God has given into his charge. He does this, firstly, because God gives him the command to do so, and the Angels most earnestly desire to do what God wishes; secondly, because he has himself an immense, personal, affectionate love for us.

a) He longs to share with us his joy, his happiness, his love, his holiness, and this with such a generosity and earnestness of desire as we selfish mortals cannot possibly understand. He labors every moment, day and night, to make us better, holier and happier.

b) Not satisfied with his own efforts on our behalf, he prays for us unceasingly and with incredible fervor to God.

What would we not give to have certainty of the prayers of a great Saint like St. Dominic, St. Francis or St. Ignatius, but we have those of an Angel, burning with the love of God and full of intense love for us, interceding constantly for us before the throne of the Most High.

God can refuse him nothing that he asks for his client, since it was God who gave him charge over us and ordered him to take every care of us.

c) This great Angel too, is constantly whispering into our ears counsels full of love and wisdom.

Our Angel may not interfere with our free will, but he can and does act on our memories, recalling vividly something we ought to do or warning us of something we ought not to do.

He acts benevolently on our imagination and on our reason, persuading us, urging us to correct our weaknesses, to fight against our evil inclinations, inspiring us with new ideals, and stimulating us to fresh and greater effort. If we do wrong, he is angry.

d) He is ever on the alert to defend us from the fierce attacks of the demons, who are our relentless foes and who use all their malice to ruin us, to tempt us, to make us sin and who stir up every sort of trouble against us.

e) Our Angels, moreover, save us from many other dangers and evils, of which we are utterly unconscious. Only in Heaven shall we come to know the favors and benefits that our Angel confers on us every day, the sorrows from which he saves us, the perils from which he snatches us.

It could not be otherwise since he is devoting to us all his angelic vigilance, all his bright intelligence. His efforts on our behalf are unceasing.

MARRIAGE

f) The Angels most especially give us help in the important events of our lives. The great bulk of men and women are called to the married state. There is nothing more vitally important for them than a *happy marriage;* nothing that ruins and wrecks their lives like an *unhappy marriage.* Now the dear Angels are more eager that their clients should obtain this great grace than father or mother, or even than they are themselves.

What happy marriages would there not be if only young men and women earnestly besought their Angels to obtain this blessing for them. Those therefore who desire a happy marriage should earnestly pray to their Angel for this grace. No one better than he can secure this blessing for them.

We read how St. Raphael obtained for Tobias a beautiful, virtuous and wealthy spouse. Our Angel can do the same for us.

SICKNESS AND SUFFERING

Another all-important fact in our lives is suffering. All must suffer, but suffering is easy to bear if only we know how to suffer, and if we have a clever nurse and an able doctor to help us when sick and if we have a kind friend who can help and console us in other troubles.

Again, our Angels are all-powerful to help us in sickness and suffering. We shall see later on how the Angels helped the martyrs to bear even with joy their cruel torments. Much more can our Angels help us to bear our little sufferings.

How many sufferers in their own homes and still more in hospitals are condemned to spend days and weeks on beds of pain and pass long interminable nights of wakefulness and agony.

What help and consolation they could have if only they knew and loved their dear Angels and called on them constantly for help, as we saw in the case of St. Gemma Galgani.

It is indeed criminal to neglect to teach boys and girls all about the Angels, for thus they are deprived during all their lives of the greatest blessings.

EXAMINATIONS

Examinations have much to say to the future happiness and welfare of boys and girls. No professor, howsoever clever he may be, can impart knowledge like our Angels, if only we ask them.

Students who are devoted to their Angels will study with far greater ease and will make far more brilliant examinations than others. Their Angels will give them a love and passion for study which is the best guarantee for acquiring knowledge.

BUSINESS MATTERS

We have frequently to embark on important business arrangements, which may bring us much gain or much loss. There are doubts and difficulties which we cannot resolve. Once more our best counsellor is our great Angel. Let us appeal to him for help and advice.

Chapter 7

IS IT BY MERE CHANCE—
OR IS IT OUR ANGEL?

We often hear the words: "I had a miraculous escape," "I escaped by a hair's breadth." But in plain truth how did we escape? It was probably our Angel who snatched us from the danger that threatened us.

Again we hear of someone who is dying, of whose life there is no hope and who suddenly takes a change for the better and gets well.

The watchers by the bedside cannot understand how it happened, neither can the doctors see a reason for the change. Was it a mere chance?

Certainly not. It was his dear Angel, who is "all-powerful," "all-loving," who intervened and saved him from a premature end. An Angel knows more about medicine and sickness than all the doctors in the world.

It is true that we cannot affirm categorically that this or that was done by the Angel if we have no proof of it, but we can say much more, *viz.*, that our Angel saves us from thousands of dangers and evils and that he confers untold benefits and favors on us, and that at *every moment* of our lives.

It is for that, and for that alone that he is standing by our sides, that he is watching over us with all his vigilant care.

Many times we ourselves prevent him from using his loving power on our behalf, because we refuse to listen to his inspirations and counsels, clinging obstinately to our evil ways, to our silly imaginings.

SOME INSTANCES

Were a person of delicate health rich enough to retain an eminent physician constantly in attendance on him, with instructions to use all his talent, to bestow all his time and to spare no expense in order to secure the improvement of his client's health, the patient would certainly attribute any betterment in his state to the unceasing care and efforts of this doctor. Yet the most eminent doctors have not the knowledge, the experience, the skill, the ability, the unrelaxing care, the eager wish to help us that our Angel has.

Why then hesitate to attribute the many extraordinarily good things that happen to us to this ever watchful Angel?

Or take the case that is occurring daily in every household of the world. Children young and full of life, giddy, of course, and possessing little sense or prudence, are given into the watchful care of a nurse, whose only task is to take care of the little ones and see that no harm comes to them.

She has nothing else to do. No one doubts that this vigilant attendant saves her charges from a thousand dangers. They may walk in streets busy with traffic, where cars, automobiles, conveyances of all kinds constantly pass, or they may walk by the side of a lake or a fast-flowing river, or on a road which borders on precipices, but they are safe. Why? Their nurse is vigilant. She keeps them from all dangers.

Yet the watchfulness of a nurse is only a faint image of the unceasing care and vigilance of a mighty Angel.

INTERESTING FACTS

A lady friend of the writer's was once travelling with her little boy of three years in an express train. The child was standing near the door of the carriage, which suddenly flew open—it had not been well closed. The boy was flung out. The mother, frantic with terror and filled with the gravest fears for the life of the little one, pulled the safety cord, but the train, which was travelling at high speed, did not pull up for a considerable time. When the rescue party reached the spot where the child had fallen, instead of finding a broken and bruised little body, as they had expected, they found the cause of their anxiety unscathed, radiant with happiness, playing as if he were in his nursery at home. The thought of all was "It was surely God's Angel who saved that child."

On another occasion, a young friend wishing to scale a high wall placed a ladder against it and proceeded to mount. At some yards from the wall, there was a deep well, about six feet in diameter, which had its sides paved from the top to the surface of the water with great stones. Suddenly, the climber found himself at the bottom of the well, standing up, unscathed.

How did this happen? The ladder must have slipped in some strange way.

In the natural course of events, he would have dashed his head against the side of the well, or fallen head foremost into the water, but except for the wetting, he escaped without the smallest scratch or bruise.

He could only think that it was his dear Angel who saved him from a horrible death, so that every day he thanks his Angel with all his heart for this favor.

A lady and her daughter were walking together on a road on the side of which was a high wall. Suddenly, the young girl stopped. Her mother repeatedly called her to come on, but she did not move. A moment afterwards the high wall crumbled and fell with an awful crash and would have certainly killed both mother and daughter had they gone only a few steps farther.

The mother, astonished at what had taken place, asked her daughter why she had stopped so suddenly, and as it proved, so opportunely.

"O, Mother!" exclaimed the girl in surprise, "did

you not see that young man who signalled to me not to go on?" Was it her Angel?

The writer once asked a venerable bishop with whom he was travelling in a motor car through a crowded city if he were afraid of accidents, since a little time before, some serious collisions had taken place.

"Oh, no," he replied. "When I get into a motor car, I at once place myself under the care of my Angel Guardian, and I feel quite safe."

A young lady who lived in a lonely country-side once assured the writer that she was never afraid, neither in daytime nor in the darkest night because she felt absolutely sure that she had her Angel with her, an Angel who loved her, an Angel "all-powerful," ready to help her. When anything happened amiss and she escaped unhurt, she instinctively thanked her Angel, for she knew full well that it was he who had kept her from harm.

Another told him that she had in her early life been very nervous and fearful, but on learning about the Angel Guardians, she was filled with boundless confidence in her Angel, so that she now enjoys perfect peace and is no longer tormented with those horrible fears.

The conduct of these two ladies should be the attitude of every good Christian.

MICHAEL'S GUARDIAN ANGEL

The following interesting fact bears, as our readers will see for themselves, the impress of truth. It happened some thirty years ago, but the account has been reprinted several times, with the personal guarantee of those who were actually present at the time of the occurrence.

In a small town in Pennsylvania, the parish priest, with the help of some nuns, was preparing the boys and girls of the parish for Confirmation. On the eve of the ceremony, the children were taken to the church to make their confessions.

One of the Sisters in attendance got annoyed at what she considered the unusual giddiness of the children. She noticed them whispering to each other and looking all in one direction, apparently at one of their companions, a little boy of ten or twelve years of age. She bade them be recollected.

On returning to the school after the confessions were over, she again reminded them that in church they must refrain from talking and whispering to each other. To her amazement, the children told her that they had seen an Angel and were quite surprised that she had not seen him too.

The tone of innocence and sincerity, and at the same time the unanimity with which all positively asserted that they had seen the Angel, impressed the good nun. In fact there seemed to be no possible doubt of what they affirmed. However, to make things still more certain and clear, she called them aside separately and diligently questioned each one as to exactly what he or she had seen when they first saw the Angel, where and what was he like.

Once more the children described, each separately, exactly what they had seen and with perfect agreement as to details. It was as follows:

One of their number, Michael, who was an excellent lad, had gone in his turn to Confession. On leaving the confessional, the children, one and all, saw a beautiful Angel, spotlessly white and radiantly beautiful, accompanying Michael, first to the altar where he knelt, and then to his place in the benches. The Angel had its wings outstretched and had an expression of tender love as it looked at Michael. At once the children, taken by surprise, whispered, "Look, look. Oh how lovely!"

The nun, more than ever convinced of the truth of what the children told her, hastened to lay the facts before the priests. These discussed the matter among themselves and then, without awakening the suspicions of the children, proceeded also to question them. They, in their turn, were deeply impressed and saw no reason for doubting what the children stated so firmly.

His Lordship the Bishop arrived in the course of the evening, and the priests gave him a full account of this consoling incident.

He also wished to have first-hand evidence, and

once more the children unwaveringly narrated to His Lordship all the facts as before.

Inquiring into Michael's behavior, he learned that he was indeed a very good and innocent boy. He was cheerful and gay, a good companion, a diligent student and, although he lived very far from the church, he attended the instructions regularly and learned his lessons with unfailing care and diligence.

The bishop, the priests and the nuns were convinced that Michael's Angel Guardian had indeed manifested his presence.

Chapter 8

THE ANGELS IN THE
SACRED SCRIPTURES

THE ANGELS IN THE OLD TESTAMENT

We find the most complete references to the Angels and proofs of their touching love for us in that best and purest of all sources, the Sacred Scriptures.

We shall, therefore, select a few of these beautiful stories, and we invite our readers to ponder on them and learn the lessons they teach. They may have read them before, but they can never drink too deeply and too often of these living waters which are the Word of God.

AN ANGEL COMFORTS AGAR

We read of how a glorious Angel appeared to Agar when she was plunged in grief and despair in the desert, seeing her son about to die a cruel death from hunger and thirst.

The Angel, full of love, consoled and comforted the sorrowing mother. He not only gave her abundance of water for herself and her son, but he filled her with great joy by assuring her that her son would become the father of a mighty race.

Every mother has a dear Angel Guardian by her side, and each of her children has one also. When children are sick, or when they cause their parents sorrow and anxiety, these mothers should remember to appeal to their holy Angels for help and consolation. One of the gravest duties of every Christian mother is to instill into the minds of her children respect and love for their Angels, to give them a full and clear comprehension of the presence of their Angel Guardians.

AN ANGEL COMES TO THE HELP OF ELIAS

In like manner one of these loving spirits came to the aid of the Prophet Elias when he was flying from Queen Jezabel, who sought to take his life.

The Prophet was worn out with sorrow and fatigue, and in the depths of his grief he lay down under the shade of a tree and besought God to allow him to die. Exhausted, he fell fast asleep.

God's dear Angel presently came and roused him from his slumber and gave him delicious bread to eat, and Heaven-sent water to slake his parching thirst.

The prophet, refreshed and invigorated by the food the Angel had given him, once more fell into a peaceful sleep.

When he had rested sufficiently, the Angel once more awoke him and bade him eat and drink again of what the Lord had sent him, for he added, "A long journey still lies before you."

Renewed in body and soul by the Angel's ministrations, the Prophet now walked for forty days
and forty nights on the strength of this angelic
food, finally reaching the goal he had set before
him, namely Mount Horeb.

Let us learn from this notable angelic intervention a lesson which will serve us in our every
need, namely that our dear Angel Guardian, who
is ever at our side, loves us with an unbounded
love and, though he may not show himself visibly
to us as he did to the Prophet, still he is nonetheless really with us, and nonetheless eager and
ready to help us if only we call on him. We must
clearly recognize the *fact* that we have an Angel
with us night and day, willing and able to comfort us in all our needs.

JUDITH WITH THE HELP OF AN ANGEL SAVES HER PEOPLE

Judith of Bethulia furnishes us with another
interesting story of angelic help.

Judith was a very beautiful and pious widow.
Her native city of Bethulia was beseiged by
Holofernes at the head of the Assyrian army. The
natives of the city were reduced to extremities
by fast-increasing want of food and drink, for the
enemy had completely cut off the water on which
the city depended for its supplies.

The unhappy rulers were already negotiating
the surrender of the city into the hands of the
enemy when this heroic woman, full of righteous

indignation, rebuked them for their want of trust in God, and determined to save the people herself. With a holy daring, she sought and obtained permission to leave the city and, with the gravest risk to her life and honor, determined to penetrate into the camp of the enemy, even into the very tent of Holofernes.

Dressing herself in costly garments, the better to gain favor with Holofernes, and taking with her a single maid, she fearlessly left the safety of the city and made her way at nightfall into the hostile camp. She was speedily seized by the enemy soldiers but, with unexampled bravery, calmly demanded of her captors to lead her to the presence of their chief, which they readily did, believing that she had a secret of great weight to impart to him.

She succeeded, as she had hoped, in winning favor with Holofernes and, biding her time until he, drunk with wine, lay on his bed in a deep sleep, she then drew his sword from its scabbard and with two mighty blows severed his head from his body. Placing her bloody trophy in a bag, she returned, under cover of night, to the gates of Bethulia and from afar cried to the watchmen on the walls to open the gates, for she said: "God is with us who has shown his power in Israel."

Great was the surprise and joy of the rulers and priests when, taking the still bleeding head of her victim from her bag, she held it up to their astonished gaze. Their lives, their city and the people were saved.

She said, "Hang the head of Holofernes on the walls, and as soon as the sun shall rise, let every man take his arms and rush out to the assault, and when you see that the enemy is fleeing, go after them without fear, for the Lord will destroy them under your feet."

The rulers followed this sage advice.

Taken by surprise at this unexpected attack by the Jews, the Assyrians sought to rouse their sleeping General, but alas, to their consternation and dismay, they found only his headless body, and seized with panic, they broke into wild flight!

The rout was complete; the pursuing Jews made a great slaughter and possessed themselves of a mighty booty. Thirty days were scarcely sufficient to gather the immense spoils.

Mindful of the brave woman, who at such imminent peril to herself had saved the city from destruction and their wives and children from the vilest of slaveries, the people sang her praises in immortal canticles, which have glorified her name for all time.

Joachim the High Priest came from Jerusalem to Bethulia with all his ancients to see Judith, and when they had come, they blessed her, as with one voice: *"Thou art the glory of Jerusalem. Thou art the joy of Israel. Thou art the honor of our people."*

Now we may ask, who helped this weak woman to carry out a plan so daring that even the bravest soldier would have hesitated and feared to undertake it?

She herself tells us that it was her holy Angel: "But as the same Lord liveth, his angel has been my keeper both going hence, and abiding there, and returning from thence hither: and the Lord hath not suffered me his handmaid to be defiled, but hath brought me back to you without pollution of sin; rejoicing for his victory, for my escape, and for your deliverance." *(Judith* 13:20).

Once more learn from Judith to place unbounded trust in our Angel Guardian.

HELIODORUS PUNISHED BY THE ANGELS

In the history of Heliodorus we have a striking proof of how God comes to the aid of those who trust Him and how He punishes His enemies.

The King of Syria, being in urgent need of money and hearing that there was much treasure in the Temple of Jerusalem, sent one of his trusty officers, named Heliodorus, to seize these treasures.

On his arrival in the Holy City, the King's messenger announced the object of his coming. The High Priest warned him that he dare not touch his money or profane the Temple. The Royal envoy made no account of the prayers of the Priest and the protests of the people, but proceeded to carry out the orders of his master.

The priests, clad in their sacerdotal vestments, prostrated themselves before the Altar, and so great was the grief and anguish depicted on the face of the High Priest that all were moved to pity and compassion.

Many too, came from their houses, praying and making public supplication to God for help in their great need.

Women and young maidens raised their hands to Heaven and implored God's all-powerful protection.

Heliodorus, intent on carrying out the orders of the King, boldly entered the treasury with his retinue, when lo! "a horse with a terrible rider on it, clad in golden armor, ran at him fiercely and struck him with its forefeet, while two young men, beautiful and strong, bright and glorious, in comely apparel, stood at either side of him and scourged him severely with rods until he fell fainting to the ground. His attendants lifted him up speechless and half dead. They placed him on a litter and carried him out without any hope for his recovery."

Filled with a holy fear and dread, they then besought the High Priest to make intercession to the Most High that his life might be spared and that he might return in safety to their King.

This the High Priest consented to do, and while he was praying, the same Angel again appeared and said to Heliodorus, "Give thanks to Onias, the High Priest, because for his sake the Lord has granted thee life."

Heliodorus, repentant and full of gratitude, offered sacrifice to God and made vows to Him who had granted him his life. He also gave thanks to Onias. Then, taking his troops, he returned to the King and testified to all men the works of the great God which he had seen with his own eyes.

When the King, still desiring to seize the treasures of the Temple, asked him who might be a fit person to send again for that purpose, he answered fearlessly, "If thou, O King, hast an enemy or traitor to thy Kingdom, send him, and thou shalt receive him again scourged, if indeed he escape at all, for there is in that place the certain power of God."

It is thus that God sends His Angels to protect His friends and punish His enemies.

Now that there is so much unrest and trouble in the world, all Christians should pray to the Holy Angels for help. If we do so, they will save us as they saved the Temple of Jerusalem.

SIDRACH, MISACH AND ABDENAGO ARE CAST INTO A FIERY FURNACE AND SAVED BY AN ANGEL

Nabuchodonosor, the all-powerful King of Babylon, built a golden statue 60 cubits high and commanded all his subjects to adore it under pain of being cast into a fiery furnace. Three Hebrew youths refused to obey and bravely told the King that their God could deliver them from his hands.

The King, in a great fury, ordered the furnace to be prepared and heated seven times more than was usual and commanded that the youths should be bound and cast into the flames.

The King's servants continued to heat the furnace with brimstone, pitch and dry sticks, but the fire did not even touch the holy youths, for an Angel came and stood by them, so that they walked in the midst of the dreadful fire, praising and blessing God; whereas, those who cast them in were caught by the flames and burned alive.

The King was astonished and exclaimed, "Did we not cast three men bound into the fire, and I see four loose and walking in the midst of the flames, and there is no hurt in them; and the form of the fourth is like the Son of God." This was the Angel God sent to help the holy youths.

He ordered the young men to come forth, and when they did so, he and his nobles saw that not even a hair of their heads had been touched by the fire.

Then the King broke forth in praise of the true God and said, "Blessed be the God of Sidrach, Misach and Abdenago, who has sent His Angel and delivered His servants who had trusted in Him. There is no other God who can save in this manner."

DANIEL IN THE LIONS' DEN

Daniel, hated by his enemies, who were jealous of him, was accused by them to King Darius for disobeying the orders he had given to adore a false god.

The King, though he loved Daniel, was constrained by these wicked men to cast him into the lions' den, for such was the law of the Medes. No time was lost. Daniel was seized and thrown to the hungry lions.

Darius, full of bitter grief, could neither eat nor sleep that night. Rising early in the morning, he hastened to the den of the lions and, calling out, asked Daniel if God had saved him. Daniel answered: "My God hath sent his Angel and hath shut up the mouths of the lions, and they have not hurt me."

The King then ordered him to be released and his enemies to be thrown to the lions. These had not well reached the bottom of the den before the lions caught and devoured them.

Then Darius the King wrote to all his people and said, "It is decreed by me that in all my empire and kingdom all men shall dread and fear the God of Daniel, for He is the living and eternal God."

Once more we see how God never fails His servants, but sends His holy Angels to take charge of them if they call on him.

ST. RAPHAEL AND TOBIAS

In the book of *Tobias,* we find a long and detailed account of how the Archangel Raphael appeared in the guise of a young man to the youthful Tobias and accompanied him on a long journey, in the course of which he conferred the most signal blessings on his young protégé.

The story of St. Raphael gives us a good idea

of the goodness and graciousness of our own dear Angel Guardian.

At the time of our story, the Jews were held in captivity by their enemies. Among the captives was a holy and just man called Tobias, who lived with his wife and only son.

This holy man prayed daily and performed many acts of charity toward his neighbors, which made him very pleasing to God, who as we shall see gave him in return an exceedingly great reward.

Tobias the elder, wishing to secure the future of his wife and son, being now blind, was forced to send his son on a long and perilous journey in order to recover a sum of money which he had loaned to a friend.

It was all-important that the youthful traveller should have a trusty companion. But where to find one? Unexpectedly, a most eligible companion appeared and professed himself ready to start at once. He gave his name as Azarias.

This God-sent friend proved to be a wise and sagacious adviser, conferring favor after favor on the young Tobias, filling his heart at the same time with admiration and gratitude.

Once, when Tobias was attacked by a great fish, he came to his aid, and by his advice Tobias extracted the heart, gall and liver of the fish, which proved to be of great medicinal value.

Next, this admirable guide and companion negotiated a most happy marriage for his young protégé, securing for him a beautiful and holy wife with a rich dowry.

Leaving Tobias with his newly-wed wife, he went himself to Rages, the city of the Medes, and recovered the money they had come to seek.

In a word, thanks to the wisdom of Azarias, Tobias returned home rejoicing, full of the good things which his guide had obtained for him and inexpressibly grateful for the services he had rendered him.

Boundless too was the joy of his dear father and mother, who had been anxiously awaiting his arrival. This joy was increased when they learned of the inestimable favor done him by his guide.

Yet another unexpected joy awaited them. Following the advice of his friend, the young Tobias anointed his father's eyes with the gall which had been extracted from the fish, and the old man recovered his sight.

RAPHAEL MAKETH HIMSELF KNOWN

Then Tobias called to him his son and said to him, "What can we give to his holy man who is come with thee?"

Tobias, answering, said to his father, "Father, what wages shall we give him, or what can be worthy of his benefits? He conducted me, and brought me safe again; he received the money of Gabelus; he caused me to have my wife; and he chased from her the evil spirit. He gave joy to her parents; myself he delivered from being devoured by the fish; thee also he hath made to see the light of heaven; and we are filled with all good things through him. What can we give him as a sufficient reward for these things?"

So the father and the son, calling him, took him aside, and began to desire him that he would vouchsafe to accept half of all things that they had brought.

Then Azarias said to them, "Bless ye the God of Heaven; give glory to Him in the sight of all that live: because He hath shewn His mercy to you. When thou didst pray with tears, and didst bury the dead, I offered thy prayer to the Lord. For I am the Angel Raphael, one of the seven who stand before the Lord."

And when they had heard these things, they were troubled; and being seized with fear, they fell upon the ground on their faces.

And the Angel said to them, "Peace be to you; fear not. For when I was with you, I was there by the will of God; bless ye Him, and sing praises to Him. It is time therefore that I return to Him that sent me: but bless ye God, and publish all His wonderful works."

And when he had said these things, he was taken from their sight, and they could see him no more.

And we? We are amazed at the goodness of God in sending His great Angel Raphael—one of the seven who stand before Him—to accompany Tobias on his journey and to abide with him for such a length of time, lavishing on him loving care and bestowing on him many and great favors.

But why not realize the no-less wonderful favor

that God has done to *each one of us,* giving us one
of His glorious Princes to be with us, not for days
only or weeks, but for all the years of our life,
shielding us from dangers and evils of every kind
and heaping on us benefits and blessings without number, never abandoning us for a single
moment.

What incredible blindness are we not guilty of
in not recognizing fully God's boundless goodness in giving us for a friend, guide and defender
a mighty Angel like Raphael.

ANGELS IN THE NEW TESTAMENT

In the New Testament too we have many beautiful examples of angelic apparitions.

An Angel came to announce to Mary that she
was to be the Mother of God. They announced
to the shepherds on the hills of Bethlehem the
birth of Jesus and sang around the stable where
Christ the King was born. An Angel warned St.
Joseph to fly into Egypt when the life of the Divine
Child was threatened by Herod, and again the
holy patriarch was informed by the Angel that
the danger had passed and that he might return
in safety to his own country. Angels ministered
to Christ in the desert. Angels assisted at His
Agony and again appeared on the day of His glorious Resurrection, and yet again when He ascended
into Heaven.

Though little mention is made of their helping the Apostles in the mighty work of evangeliz-

ing the world, yet we may rest assured that they took an active part in this divine work. We shall quote two occasions in which mention is made of their cooperation with the Apostles.

ST. PETER DELIVERED BY AN ANGEL

King Herod Agrippa, when he put the Apostle St. James to death, saw that this pleased the Jews, and therefore had St. Peter likewise arrested.

Casting him into a loathsome dungeon, he set four companies of soldiers to guard him, intending to take his life after the feast of the Pasch. In the meantime, the faithful offered up unceasing prayers for his deliverance. Their prayers were heard. One night, the Apostle's prison was suddenly filled with a bright light, and an Angel appeared to him. Peter, fastened with chains, was sleeping among the soldiers. The Angel, touching his side, awoke him and bade him arise. The chains fell from his hands. "Gird thyself and put on thy sandals," said the Angel, "and follow me." Peter followed and issued from his prison, not sure at first whether it was not all a dream. After passing the first and second guardhouses, they came to the iron gate that opened to the city. It flew open of its own accord, and going out, the Angel disappeared as soon as they had gained the top of the street.

Peter coming to himself exclaimed, "I see now that the Lord has sent His Angel, who has delivered me out of Herod's hands." He went immediately to the house where his brethren were assembled in prayer for his delivery.

AN ANGEL APPEARS TO ST. PAUL

St. Paul, being accused by the Jews, who after his conversion were his declared enemies, appealed to Caesar by his right as a Roman citizen. He was therefore put on board a vessel bound for Italy, along with many prisoners and several merchants. All were under the charge of Julius, a centurion, who paid marked respect to the Apostle. The passengers numbered in all two hundred seventy-six.

During the voyage a dreadful storm arose, and for several days neither the sun nor the stars were visible. All seemed lost, so that the cargo was thrown into the sea in the hope of lessening the danger. But in vain. All would certainly have perished had it not been for the prayers of the Apostle.

In answer to his prayers, a glorious Angel appeared to him and assured him of his safety and that of his fellow passengers. Thereupon, St. Paul addressed all on board in these words: "Be of good courage. None of ye shall perish, for the Angel of the Lord whom I serve has appeared to me this night."

WHY ARE WE NOT HELPED MORE BY THE ANGELS?

Remark, dear reader, that the Angels came to help the Apostles in answer to fervent prayer.

Frequently, we do not receive the help of the Angels, simply because we do not pray. In all our needs we should pray fervently to the Angels, and we shall receive their "all-powerful" help.

Chapter 9

THREE GREAT PRINCES

The three Angels of whom special mention is made in the Sacred Scriptures are St. Michael, St. Gabriel and St. Raphael.

We must strive to learn all we can about these mighty Princes and do our best to honor them, which we can easily do without unduly multiplying our prayers. In return for the love we show them, we may rest assured that we shall receive abundant graces.

ST. MICHAEL

The first fact we learn concerning this great Prince is that in the mighty combat which took place in Heaven, when the bad Angels fell away from their allegiance to God, Michael sounded his war cry: "Who is like to God," and immediately, joined by the good Angels, he drove Satan and his legions from Heaven and plunged them into the depths of Hell.

Next, we hear his praises from no less an authority than his brother Angel, St. Gabriel, who speaking to the Prophet Daniel, says, "Michael, who is your Prince," "Michael, who is a great Prince created for the children of your people," and again, "Michael, who is one of the first among Princes."

St. Thomas says of him, "Michael is the breath of the Redeemer's spirit who will, at the end of the world, combat and destroy Antichrist, as he did Lucifer in the beginning."

St. Michael was the protector and defender of God's chosen people.

He came with the Israelites from Egypt and accompanied them through the desert. He it was who gave them, from God, the Ten Commandments, and during the thousands of years that elapsed before the coming of Christ, he was their champion and defender. Though express mention of him is made only a few times, yet owing to his office as their appointed friend and defender, we know that he never abandoned God's people but took an important part in all that concerned them.

He is now the defender of the Catholic Church and of all the faithful, whom he defends against the constant assaults of the devil. He is invoked in sickness and most especially at the hour of death, when his "all-powerful" help is so much needed, for then it is that Satan makes his last and fiercest attack on the Christian soul, seeking with craft and cunning, with fears and despair to drag it down to Hell.

In the prayers formerly said by the priest and people after Mass, there was a special and beautiful prayer to St. Michael imploring his help for the Church. It runs as follows:

Saint Michael, the Archangel, defend us in the day of battle; be our safeguard against the wickedness and snares of the devil. May God rebuke him we humbly pray; and do thou, O Prince of the heavenly host, by the power of God, thrust down to Hell Satan and with him all the wicked spirits, who wander through the world seeking the ruin of souls. Amen.

We should make it a sacred duty to join *fervently* in this important prayer.

In our morning and evening prayers we invoke St. Michael when saying the *Confiteor,* but we should try to do so with more devotion and confidence. Many do not even think of what they are saying.

St. Michael has been honored from the earliest times in many countries. The Emperor Constantine, grateful for the victories gained over his enemies, which he attributed to the protection of St. Michael, built a magnificent church near Constantinople in honor of the Archangel which he called Michaelion. It became a place of pilgrimage, and many sick and infirm were cured in it by the intercession of the Archangel.

Constantine's successors erected no less than fifteen churches in Constantinople itself to St. Michael.

In Rome churches were also built and dedicated to St. Michael as far back as 494.

The Archangel appeared to the Bishop of Siponto, on Monte Gargano, in the Kingdom of Naples, where a beautiful church was dedicated to him. This became a place of great devotion and attracted many pilgrims.

In France, he appeared on Mont St. Michel, where there still exists a famous sanctuary consecrated to the Archangel.

In Egypt, the Christians dedicated their food-giving river, the Nile, to St. Michael, and on the 12th of every month they held a special celebration in his honor, and this celebration was kept with marked solemnity in the month of June, when the river begins to rise.

When Germany was converted, the cult to the pagan god Woden was replaced by devotion to St. Michael, and as a result there are to be seen numerous chapels dedicated to the Archangel in the mountain districts of that country.

In England the feast of Michaelmas used to be celebrated with great rejoicing, the favorite dish of the day being the roast goose.

Now it is mainly known as a legal term, the day marking what is called in law, the Michaelmas term.

St. Michael has appeared at different times to those who needed his help and invoked his aid. A most notable example was when he assisted St.

Joan of Arc in the extraordinary mission given her by God of aiding the French King to restore peace and prosperity to his kingdom and expel his enemies from its shores.

ST. MICHAEL AT THE HOUR OF DEATH

We read in *The Book of Similitudes* of St. Anselm that a religious of this monastery, on the point of death, was dreadfully assaulted by the devil, who reproached him at first because of the sins he had committed previous to his Baptism, for the monk had received this Sacrament when already advanced in years. The poor man knew not how to reply and was very much troubled until St. Michael, who had come to his assistance, answered that all the sins he had committed before Baptism were remitted in that Sacrament. The evil spirit then urged several sins of his committed after Baptism. The Archangel replied that these had been washed away in the general confession he made before his religious profession, and that the dying man should trust in the divine mercy. Satan at last opposed to him the many offenses and negligences in his life subsequent to religious profession. As the good monk said nothing in defense, St. Michael declared that all his sins were forgiven him, because he had confessed them and satisfied for them by good works, especially by obedience, and that if anything remained it was expiated by his patience under the sufferings of a sickbed.

At these words the devil departed in confusion, and the good religious, with confident hope, sweetly gave up his soul to God.

We all must die, and we all must be prepared for the fierce attacks of the devil at this dreadful hour. Hence every Christian should make sure of having St. Michael's help at the hour of death. This we can do by being devoted to the great Archangel during our lives.

CHILDREN RAISED TO LIFE BY ST. MICHAEL

The King of Dacia, Mulhoares, was gravely ill and suffered all the more because he had no heir to his throne. His children had all died. He was counselled to have recourse to St. Michael.

The King followed this sage advice, and some time after twins were born to his wife. Alas, a new trial awaited him. These children also died!

Full of lively faith, the King ordered the bodies of the children to be taken to the church and placed before the altar of St. Michael, and he and his people besought the great Archangel to come to their aid. Lo, St. Michael appeared and spoke to the King: "I am Michael, whom you and your people have invoked, and I have presented your petition to God who is pleased to restore life to your children. Behold them alive, and I and the other Angels will watch over them. God wishes, too, to cure you, but you must thank the Angel who is Prince of your kingdom. That you may love him, I will now show him to you."

A most beautiful Angel then appeared, clothed in royal robes, with a crown of gold on his head. He blessed the King, who was instantly restored to health.

HOW TO HONOR ST. MICHAEL?

1st. By frequently repeating this short prayer: **"Glorious St. Michael, Prince of the Heavenly Court, pray for us now and at the hour of our death."**

2nd. By invoking his aid in sickness.

3rd. If we find it hard to conquer a temptation, or correct some fault, let us pray to St. Michael, who will assuredly help us to overcome the most violent temptation—and the most inveterate.

4th. By having a little picture of St. Michael in our prayerbook, saying each time we see it, "Glorious St. Michael, I love you."

ST. GABRIEL

This great Archangel bears the glorious title of *"The Angel of the Incarnation,"* for it was he whom God chose to act as Ambassador to men in all that pertained to this stupendous Mystery.

He foretold to Daniel the exact time of the birth of Christ.

He announced to Zacharias the birth of St. John the Baptist, the Precursor of the Redeemer.

However his most glorious mission—one that

links him inseparably with the Incarnation and
wins for him the affection and love of all Christian peoples—was when he came as divine messenger from the Most Holy Trinity to announce
to the Virgin Mary that God had chosen her to
be the Mother of His Divine Son.

Millions and millions of Catholics all the world
over, in every land, in every language, repeat daily
and every moment of the day the very words that
St. Gabriel spoke to Mary. Saying the *Hail Mary*
they offer her over and over again the joys and
happiness of that forever blessed moment when
the Eternal Son of God took flesh in her most
pure womb and made her His Holy Mother.

Every time, then, that we say the *Hail Mary,* let
it be our distinct intention to offer to Our Lady
all the graces and joys that St. Gabriel offered
her in the Annunciation: *"Hail full of grace, the
Lord is with thee, blessed art thou among women."*

Every time we say the first Joyful Mystery of
the Rosary, the Annunciation, we do the same,
but in a still more solemn and complete manner.

Again, when three times a day we say the
Angelus, we fill the heart of our Blessed Mother
with unspeakable joy, and she in return pours
down oceans of graces upon us. A great Saint
once said that those who say the *Angelus* devoutly
are already halfway to Heaven.

What pleasure, what glory, too, do we not give
the glorious Archangel Gabriel by repeating
lovingly his very words, the words he brought from
the Holy Trinity, the words that gave us the great

news of our Redemption.

But many, many Christians are so forgetful or so negligent that when they recite these most beautiful prayers, they neither think of the delight and gladness they give to most Holy Mary, nor have they any idea of the boundless pleasure they give to St. Gabriel.

Therefore, dear Reader, in the future, *a)* when saying the *Hail Mary,* *b)* the first Joyful Mystery of the Rosary, *viz.* the Annunciation, *c)* when saying thrice every day the *Angelus,* remember to say them in union with St. Gabriel.

Though his name is not expressly mentioned, we may well believe what Tradition tells us, that it was St. Gabriel who announced to the shepherds on the hills of Bethlehem the birth of our Sweet Lord; that it was he, too, who led the multitude of blessed spirits who sang around the Crib the heavenly song, *"Gloria in excelsis Deo et pax hominibus bonae voluntatis."* ("Glory to God in the highest, and peace to men of good will.")

It was he too who comforted and consoled dear St. Joseph in his sorrow, who warned the holy Patriarch to fly with the Divine Child and His Blessed Mother into Egypt and who again bade him return, when Herod had died.

Lastly, it was St. Gabriel who came to comfort the Son of God in His great Agony in the Garden of Olives.

When saying the first Sorrowful Mystery, Christ's Agony in the Garden, let us offer Jesus our pity and compassion in union with dear St. Gabriel.

By following these simple suggestions, we will give the Archangel the greatest honor and he will help us to say more fervently and lovingly these prayers which perhaps we have hitherto recited coldly or tepidly.

In return for this simple devotion we shall make the glorious Archangel our most powerful and loving friend.

ST. RAPHAEL

The name "Raphael" signifies "health" or "medicine of God."

We have already spoken of the loving care which he showed to the young Tobias. Many believe, with great reason, that it was he who so often miraculously healed the wounds suffered by the martyrs and comforted them in the torments inflicted on them. He is the gracious Spirit who, with benevolent care, brings back so many travellers safe to their native land. Let us not, then, fail to invoke his protection whenever we undertake a journey, and also when we are sick, for he also works wonderful cures. Some interesting facts are related of this Archangel.

STORIES OF ST. RAPHAEL

St. Cyriaca, also called Dominica, because she was born on a Sunday, who was martyred at Nicomedia under the Emperor Maximian (in the

4th century), heard a voice from Heaven saying to her during her conflict: "Well done, Cyriaca! Victorious one! Christ the King has heard your prayers: be strong and resolute. I who am speaking to you am the Archangel Raphael, and I am sent by our Saviour to make you vigorous and to give you this message from the Most High: Because you have placed your confidence in Christ, you will glorify the Lord who strengthens you." This Saint's feast is kept on May 18th.

St. John of God cultivated a remarkable devotion to St. Raphael. Hence the Archangel once visited the poor in the hospital at Granada when John had gone out to fetch water. Another time, when the sick people were short of bread, he brought them some; and a third time, he helped John to carry home a poor man. On this occasion he made himself known. In fact, as the writer of St. John's life says, he acted toward that hospital as he did toward the young Tobias, whom he accompanied on his journey and protected in every peril.

The Carmelite nun Blessed Mary of the Angels honored St. Raphael in a special manner and endeavored to spread devotion to him by every means in her power. In return she received many and great favors.

Because Sister Mary Francis of the Third Order of St. Francis was always ill, it pleased God to confide her specially to the care of St. Raphael. In 1789 he appeared to her in such a beautiful form that she was quite taken by surprise and could not speak. He told her that he had come to cure her. Next day she was quite well, owing to his ministrations. On another occasion, when on account of a swollen vein which gave her such trouble that she was unable to make the least effort, he generously came to her assistance.

Once when Father Francis Bianchi was talking to her, he became conscious of a remarkable and most fragrant perfume around him, and on asking for an explanation of it, she replied that it was caused by the Angel Raphael, who was present, but whom the Father did not see.

In 1315 a young novice repaired to a convent of the Order of St. Dominic, desiring to assume the habit. He was subject to the falling sickness, but did not mention this on being admitted into the monastery. It was, however, soon known, for when the fit seized him, he would fall on the ground and lie there insensible for three hours. For this reason, after a trial of twelve months, the religious could not receive him among the brethren, but out of compassion, sent him to another house of the Order, where he was provided for. The same evil again tormenting him, a brother named Richard DuPont began to pray for his relief. The Angel Raphael, appearing to Richard in his sleep, told him that if the novice would make a vow to fast on the first day of every week in honor of the Angels, his infirmity would be removed, the Angel adding that he was Raphael, whom God had sent to cure him. The patient, on hearing the glad news, made the vow, and lo, he fell down in his fit and saw the Angel arouse him, with the assurance that he was cured! Nor did he ever after suffer any affliction. Admitted to make his religious profession, he lived to be a holy priest.

In a learned work published in France on the Angels, we read that a certain wealthy man of the city of Orleans, when setting out on a pilgrimage to the Sanctuary of St. James, recommended himself particularly to the Angel Raphael, whose devotion he cherished as the protector of travellers. On his journey he lost his way, and as he was approaching a wood, perceived some robbers evidently about to attack him. Turning back, he fled in haste and was suddenly joined by a person who asked him why he ran away. The pilgrim pointed toward the brigands, but the unknown companion bade him not to fear. By this time they had reached the bank of a river, and as there was no bridge or boat of any kind, the unfortunate traveller was more terrified than ever. He thought that his companion had deceived him, and seeing the robbers approaching, he invoked the aid of St. Raphael. Presently, he found himself transported across the river and thus delivered from his enemies. At the same time, his companions disappeared!

The pilgrim then continued his journey. On his return, arriving near the same forest, he feared to fall in with the robbers, but wearied and exhausted, he fell asleep under a tree. The companion who had before borne him over the river, now appearing to him in a vision, made known to him that he was the Angel Raphael, to whose care he had confided himself, and who preserved him on his way from every peril. The pilgrim, awaking, was surprised to find himself within a league of Orleans.

Chapter 10

THE ANGELS AND THE MARTYRS

We are justly surprised at seeing the marvellous constancy of the Martyrs in the midst of most cruel sufferings. Their bodies were torn with iron hooks or burned in slow fires; their bones were dislocated on the rack or broken with iron hammers.

Even young boys and gentle girls were subjected to every imaginable torture, which they bore with such patience and courage that the spectators, and even their brutal executioners themselves, were lost in amazement.

How was it possible, one may ask, for poor weak mortals, just like ourselves, to endure such fearful torments? We cannot keep our hands in boiling water for one moment, nor can we keep even the tip of our fingers in the flame of a little candle. How was it that the martyrs behaved with such heroic fortitude when their whole bodies were being racked with hooks, or torn with lashes, or burned in slow fires? The explanation is that God sustained them and sent His Angels to help them. These blessed Spirits filled the Martyrs with superhuman strength, soothed their pains, and consoled them in their suffering, so that it became easy and even pleasant for them to bear the torments that their brutal enemies invented with such fiendish ingenuity.

What a lesson for us! Why do we not call with confidence on our dear Angels in our sufferings? They are only too eager to come to our assistance.

St. Theodosius, as Rufinus tells us, was asked after enduring horrible torments for the Faith, if he had not felt intensely those dreadful pains? "In the beginning yes," he replied, "but an Angel soon came to my side and refreshed my burning wounds. When the torture ceased, I was sorry, for then the Angel went away, and I no longer enjoyed his sweet presence."

St. Agnes. When the dear Virgin, St. Agnes, refused to adore the false idols of Rome, the impious judge ordered her to be taken to a bad house and to be insulted. An Angel appeared, and no one dared to harm her. One, more wicked than the others, finally attempted to insult the young Martyr, and he was stricken blind by an Angel.

His companions, terrified, begged St. Agnes to pray for him, which she did, and his sight was restored.

When St. Dorothy was condemned to death for her faith, a young man named Theophilus, hearing her speak of Paradise, laughed with scorn and said to her: "Send me some fruit and flowers from the garden of your Heavenly Spouse." She promised to do so.

When she reached the place of execution, an Angel in the form of a young man approached her with some delicious fruit and flowers, to whom she said: "Take them to Theophilus and say that I send them to him." Theophilus was stricken dumb with amazement, for the weather was cold, and there were no flowers or fruit to be seen anywhere. He became a Christian and died for Christ.

St. Cecilia belonged to an illustrious Roman family. She became a Christian and dedicated her virginity to our Lord Jesus Christ. Her parents, however, insisted on espousing her to a young Roman noble gentleman called Valerian.

On the day of their marriage, Cecilia spoke frankly to her husband and told him that she had pledged her virginity to God and was defended by an Angel who would certainly punish him if he did not respect her pledge.

Valerian, who was a pagan, asked to see the Angel, and Cecilia replied that he could do so if he became a Christian. To this he consented and sought out Pope Urban, who was hidden in the catacombs, owing to the fierce persecution then raging against the Church.

The Holy Father received him kindly, instructed him and baptized him.

On returning home, he at once saw the Angel, resplendent with beauty, who placed a crown on his head and another on that of Cecilia, saying:

"Be worthy to keep these precious crowns; I bring them to you from Heaven."

Valerian was filled with joy and told all that had happened to his brother Tiburcio, also a pagan. He too, desirous of seeing the Angel, received instruction and after Baptism had the same happiness and was enraptured by the sweetness and majesty of the blessed Spirit.

All three, later on, laid down their lives for the love of Christ, assisted by their holy Angels.

St. Eulalia. The story of St. Eulalia, the child Martyr, is another beautiful instance of how the Angels helped the Martyrs.

This dear little girl, only twelve years old, was brought before the brutal judges, who used every means in their power to terrify her and compel her to deny the religion of Jesus Christ. They threatened her with the most awful torments and showed her the instruments of torture with which the executioners were going to tear her flesh and break her bones. But three Angels came to her assistance and so consoled and encouraged her that she was glad to have to suffer for her dear Lord.

The Angels told her what to answer the judges, who were confounded at the wisdom and courage of the child.

She saw the Angels, who were radiant with beauty and lovingly consoled her. One said to her: "Suffer for Our Lord Jesus Christ. He loves you with an infinite love."

Another said to her: "Suffer, dear Child, for soon you will be one of us and will rejoice with us forever in Heaven."

A third added: "Suffer with courage, Eulalia, for you will save many souls by your constancy and example."

And then all three affectionately said: "Don't you wish to be our dear little Sister?"

The words of the Angels filled the heart of Eulalia with such joy and strength that she exclaimed: "O, dear Lord, what joy to have written on my body in letters of blood the signs of Your sufferings and wounds!"

Finally, she was burned alive, and her soul was borne by Angels heavenwards.

ST. VINCENT MARTYR

In the glorious history of the tens of thousands of Martyrs who fearlessly died in defense of their faith, the story of St. Vincent is one of the most wonderful.

St. Vincent was a young Spanish nobleman who was seized by orders of Dacian, the Proconsul, in company with his bishop, Valerius.

Valerius was sent into exile, but St. Vincent was condemned to the most awful torments.

He was first stretched on the rack. His hands and feet were drawn by cords and pullies till they were almost pulled from their sockets. Whilst in this posture, his flesh was brutally torn off with iron hooks.

Vincent only smiled. Dacian thought that the executioners spared him and caused them to be beaten. Exasperated by their punishment, they returned, resolved to satisfy the cruelty of their master, who incited them to exert their utmost strength and cruelty. They began with fresh vigor to rend and tear his body, which they did with such barbarity that his bones and bowels were exposed to sight. The more his body was mangled, the greater was the joy on his countenance.

The judge, seeing the streams of blood which flowed from all the parts of his body and the frightful condition to which he was reduced, was obliged to confess with astonishment that the courage of this heroic Christian had vanquished him. He begged the Saint for his own sake that if he would not offer sacrifice to the gods, he would at least give up the sacred books to be burned. The Martyr refused with scorn to do so.

Dacian, now more incensed than ever, condemned him to further tortures, *viz.,* to be roasted on a kind of gridiron. The Saint went with joy to the frightful engine so as to get there before his executioners, such was his desire to suffer. He cheerfully mounted the iron bed, in which the bars were framed like scythes, full of sharp spikes made red-hot by the fire underneath. On this dreadful gridiron the Martyr was stretched at full length and bound fast.

While one part of his body was broiling over the fire, the other was tortured by the application of red-hot plates of iron. His wounds were rubbed with salt, which the activity of the fire forced the deeper into his flesh. All the parts of his body were tormented in this manner, one after the other, and each several times over. The melted fat dropping from the flesh nourished and increased the flames, which instead of tormenting, seemed, as St. Austin says, to give the Martyr new vigor and courage. The more he suffered, the greater seemed to be the inward joy and consolation of his soul.

The rage and confusion of the tyrant exceeded all bounds; he was unable to contain himself and was continually inquiring what Vincent did and what he said, and he was always answered that he suffered with joy in his countenance and seemed every moment to acquire new strength and resolution as he lay unmoved on the fire. His eyes were turned toward Heaven, his mind calm, and his heart fixed on God in continual prayer.

At last, by the command of the Proconsul, he was thrown into a dungeon, and his wounded body laid on the floor strewn with broken potsherds, which opened afresh his ghastly wounds and cut anew his poor flesh. His legs were set in wooden stocks, stretched very wide, and strict orders were given that he should be left without food or drink, and no one should be admitted to see or speak to him.

How was Vincent able to endure these fiendish tortures with such joy?

Again we find the answer: God sustained him and sent His Angels to help and to comfort him. With these, he sang the praises of his God.

The gaoler, seeing through the chinks of the door the prison filled with light and the Saint walking and praising God, was converted and baptized.

At this news Dacian chafed, and even wept with rage. He now resorted to kindness, in the hope of changing Vincent's determination and ordered that some repose should be allowed the prisoner. The faithful were permitted to see him, and coming in great numbers wiped and kissed his wounds, and dipped cloths in his blood, which they kept as an assured protection for themselves and their posterity. After this, a soft bed was prepared for him, upon which he was no sooner laid than he expired and was carried by the Angels in triumph to Heaven.

Dacian commanded his body to be thrown into a marshy field among rushes, but a raven defended it from wild beasts and birds of prey.

It was then tied to a great stone and cast into the sea, but it was miraculously brought back to the shore and shown to two Christians. They laid it in a little chapel outside the walls of Valentia, where God honored these relics with many miracles, as St. Austin tells us.

Afterwards the relics were brought to Lisbon, where they are honored in the Cathedral Church. St. Vincent is the Patron Saint of this city.

ST. LAWRENCE

Who has not heard of the glorious martyrdom of St. Lawrence, so like in many respects to that of St. Vincent?

He too was born in Spain but went to Rome, where he was the close friend of the Holy Pontiff, St. Sixtus, whom he served in the capacity of deacon.

When St. Sixtus was seized, Lawrence was deeply grieved that he could not die together with his dear Master. "Where are you going, my Father," he exclaimed, "without your son; where without your minister?" St. Sixtus replied: "Grieve not, my son. I who am now old and weak am called to suffer little; you are reserved for great combats, which will be told for all time."

This prophecy was fulfilled to the letter.

St. Lawrence sold the goods belonging to the Church and gave the money to the poor. He was then seized and subjected to the most cruel tortures, one after another. At the sight of his marvellous courage, many were converted, including one of the guards, called Hypolitus.

His garments were torn off, and he was barbarously scourged. After this his executioners showed him the awful instruments of torture with which they were about to inflict on his already lacerated body the most excruciating pains. All their efforts were, however, in vain. Nothing could shake his patience or wring from him a cry or a groan. Instead, he smiled at his tormentors.

The judge now ordered him to be stretched on the rack, so that his joints were dislocated. Next, he was beaten with whips armed with leaden balls, and his flesh was so horribly mangled that he felt that he was dying.

But a voice was heard telling him that he was still reserved for greater trials. This voice caused great surprise to the bystanders, and one of the soldiers, called Romanus, was much impressed. He saw a beautiful Angel wiping the sweat from the Martyr's brow and the blood from his wounds, thus giving him immense joy.

The sight of this glorious Angel and the fortitude of Lawrence converted the soldier, who was baptized and, in his own turn, died for Christ.

Beside himself with anger, the judge commanded Lawrence to be stretched on an iron gridiron beneath which a slow fire was constantly kept burning.

The Martyr bade the executioners to turn him, saying, "This side is now roasted." They did so. After a little while he said to them, "Now I am fully cooked, come and eat my flesh." And so saying, he lifted his eyes to Heaven and breathed forth his pure soul into the hands of God.

The cruel judge and the brutal executioners were lost in amazement. They had never witnessed such extraordinary courage in the midst of such appalling torments.

ST. VENANTIUS AND THE ANGELS

St. Venantius was a boy of fifteen years, simple and modest in bearing, a devout Christian and of indomitable courage in the practice of his faith.

The persecution against the Christians had broken out afresh, and Venantius learned that the pagan authorities were seeking to seize him. Far from flying from the danger, as he could easily have done, he went straight to the judge and declared himself a follower of Christ.

Instead of admiring the heroism of the youth, the brutal judge became infuriated, ordered him to be seized, stripped of his garments and beaten so mercilessly that he would certainly have died under the blows showered on him by the savage executioners, had it not been for a glorious Angel, full of beauty and strength, who severed the ropes that bound him and hurled back at the same time his tormentors.

Venantius did not seek to escape. The Angel had imbued him with fresh courage and an earnest desire to die for Christ. Oh, for the Martyr's crown!

The judge now ordered him to be hung up by the heels over a fire, with his head down and his mouth forced open, so that he would be suffocated by the fumes. With admirable calm and courage, he resisted these new efforts to make him renounce his faith.

Seeing his immovable constancy in these sufferings, the judge had recourse to promises and rewards and sent his agent, Anatole, to use all his ingenuity to induce the heroic boy to renounce Christ.

Venantius, full of a holy indignation, drove the messenger from his presence. On hearing of the failure of his agent, the judge ordered the executioners to break the teeth and jaws of Venantius with iron hammers and then to throw him into a filthy pit where he would die of suffocation.

The Angel again appeared and gently drew the Martyr from the foul pit.

Venantius once more stood before the judge, who fell headlong from the tribunal and died, exclaiming, "The God of Venantius is the only true God."

The governor of the city, on being made aware of the awful death of his iniquitous judge, gave orders to throw Venantius to the lions, but to the surprise of the people, the wild beasts lay down at his side, gentle as lambs. The martyr, availing himself of the opportunity, raised his voice and preached to the multitude that thronged the circus the religion and love of Jesus Christ, whom even the wild beasts had honored and obeyed.

Porphyrius, a holy and fearless priest, presented himself to the governor and told him that he had seen in a vision all those whom Venantius had converted, wearing glorious crowns and enjoying immense glory and happiness; whereas, his persecutors were plunged into dark and dreadful dungeons, into which the governor himself would soon be cast.

The wretched man refused to listen to the warning and commanded Porphyrius to be slain and Venantius to be dragged over rugged ground strewn with thorns and thistles.

In the course of this new torture, the executioners became weary and consumed with thirst, and Venantius caused a spring of fresh water to spring up, in which they quenched their thirst. Many of them, full of gratitude to Venantius and admiring his wonderful powers, were at once converted and were, together with Venantius, beheaded.

Following the execution, a fearful storm burst over the city, and the impious governor attempted to fly, but died most miserably.

These glorious martyrs, whose history we have just given, are only a few of the **millions of men and women** who have given their lives and shed their blood amidst appalling sufferings in defense of their faith and for the love of Jesus Christ.

The Holy Angels assisted not a few, but all of them, to bear not only with courage but even with joy the barbarous tortures to which they were subjected.

Suffering is the share of all in this vale of tears. Suffering is our little share in the Passion of Our Dear Lord.

We repeat now what we have already said, because it is so important, *viz.,* that one of the best means to make our sufferings light and easy is to ask our Angel Guardian to help us. It is for that that he is ever by our side, ready to aid us in every way, ready to obtain all favors for us from God, ready to share with us his own immense happiness.

Oh, if we only had confidence and unbounded trust in our Angel, he would save us from a thousand evils and obtain for us a thousand joys and blessings!

If the Angels could help the Martyrs in their awful sufferings, much more can they help us in our little sorrows.

Chapter 11

THE CHRONICLES OF THE DOMINICAN ORDER

We find many beautiful accounts of angelic apparitions in the chronicles of the Order of St. Dominic.

ST. DOMINIC AND THE ANGELS

The following is a brief account of how the Angels appeared to St. Dominic himself and his friars.

When the Friars were still living near the church of St. Sixtus and were about one hundred in number, on a certain day the blessed Dominic commanded Father John of Calabria and Father Albert of Rome to go into the city to beg alms. They did so, but without success, from the morning even till the third hour of the day. They then returned to the convent and were already hard by the church of St. Anastasia, when they were met by a certain woman who had a great devotion to the Order; and seeing that they had nothing with them, she gave them a loaf. "I would not," she said, "that you should go back quite empty-handed." As they went on a little further, they met a man who asked them very importunately for charity. They excused themselves, saying they had nothing themselves; but the man only begged the more earnestly. Then they said one to another, "What can we do with only one loaf? Let us give it to him for the love of God." So they gave him the loaf, and immediately they lost sight of him! Now, when they were come to the convent, the Blessed Father, to whom the Holy Spirit had meanwhile revealed all that had passed, came out to meet them, saying to them with a joyful air: "Children, you have nothing?" They replied, "No, Father," and they told him all that had happened and how they had given the loaf to the poor man. Then said he, "It was an Angel of the Lord; the Lord will know how to provide for His own. Let us go and pray." Thereupon he entered the church and having come out again after a little space, he bade the brethren call the community to the refectory. They replied to him saying, "But Holy Father, how is it you would have us call them, seeing that there is nothing to give them to eat?" The Blessed Father, however, caused Brother Roger to be summoned and commanded him to assemble the brethren for dinner, for the Lord would provide for their wants. Then they prepared the tables and placed the cups, and at a given signal, all the community entered the refectory. The Blessed Father gave the benediction, and everyone being seated, Father Henry the Roman began to read. Meanwhile, the Blessed Dominic was praying, his hands being joined together on the table;

and lo, suddenly, even as he had promised them, by the inspiration of the Holy Ghost, two beautiful young men, ministers of the Divine Providence, appeared in the midst of the refectory, carrying loaves in two white cloths which hung from their shoulders before and behind. They began to distribute the bread, beginning at the lower rows, one at the right hand, and the other at the left, placing before each brother one whole loaf of admirable beauty. Then, when they were come to the Blessed Dominic and had in like manner placed an entire loaf before him, they bowed their heads and disappeared, without anyone knowing, even to this day, whence they came or whither they went. And the Blessed Dominic said to his brethren, "My brethren, eat the bread which the Lord has sent you." Then he told the servers to pour out some wine. But they replied, "Holy Father, there is none." Then the Blessed Dominic, full of the spirit of prophecy, said to them, "Go to the vessel and pour out to the brethren the wine which the Lord has sent them." They went there and found, indeed, that the vessel was filled up to the brim with an excellent wine, which they hastened to bring. And Dominic said, "Drink, my brethren, of the wine which the Lord has sent you." They ate, therefore, and drank as much as they desired, both that day, and the next, and the day after that. But after the meal of the third day, the Holy Father caused them to give what remained of the bread and wine to the poor and would not allow that it should be kept in the house. During these three days no one went to seek alms because God had sent them bread and wine in abundance.

At a later date the Angels appeared in a similar way a second time to the Holy Patriarch and his friars and gave them to eat in abundance.

On a third occasion, St. Dominic had to go from the Convent of St. Sixtus outside of Rome to the Convent of Santa Sabina in Rome. But Father Tancred, the prior of the brethren, and Odo, the prior of the sisters and all the friars, and the prioress, with the sisters, tried to detain him, saying: "Holy Father, it is very late, and it is not expedient for you to go." Nevertheless, he refused to do as they wished, and said, "The Lord wills me to depart and will send His Angel with me." Then he took for his companions Tancred and Odo and set out. And being arrived at the church door, in order to depart, behold, according to the words of the Blessed Dominic, a young man of great beauty presented himself, having a staff in his hand, as if ready for a journey. Then the Blessed Dominic made his companions go on before him, the young man going first and he last, and so they came to the door of the Church of Santa Sabina, which they found shut. The young man leaned against the door, and immediately it opened; he entered first, then the brethren, and then the Blessed Dominic. And the young men went out, and the door again shut, and

Brother Tancred said: "Holy Father, who was the young man who came with us?" And he replied, "My son, it was an Angel of God, whom He sent to guard us."

ST. THOMAS AQUINAS GIRDED BY THE ANGELS WITH THE CINCTURE OF PURITY

When St. Thomas Aquinas, who came of a very noble and illustrious family—royal blood flowed in his veins—joined the Dominican Order, his family was furious at his action.

His brothers, who were officers in the army of Emperor Frederick, seized him and put him in prison in one of the family castles.

Here they did their best to persuade him to leave the Order and cast off the white habit, a course which he calmly but firmly refused to adopt.

His captors then tore the habit from his shoulders and threw the pieces with contempt on the floor. The Saint quietly picked up the fragments of his habit and folded them reverently.

The two brothers then planned a truly diabolical method of attack. They contrived to introduce into the prison a beautiful but abandoned woman, with the promise of a large reward if she could succeed in shaking the virtue and resolution of their brother. The very first words of the treacherous visitor opened the eyes of Thomas to a sense of his danger. He shuddered, looked up to Heaven, and seizing a blazing brand from the hearth, drove the wretched creature from the room. Then, trembling at the thought of the danger he had escaped, he traced a cross on the wall with the smouldering brand and, kneeling down, made an act of intense gratitude for his deliverance and a fervent consecration of his whole being to God. While thus praying, he fell into an ecstatic sleep, during which two Angels from Heaven appeared to him, and girded him with a miraculous cord, saying at the same time these words: "We have come from God, to invest thee with the girdle of perpetual chastity. The Lord has heard thy prayer, and that which human frailty could never merit is assured to thee by the irrevocable gift of God." This was no dream, but a reality, for the Angels girded him so tightly that the pain awoke St. Thomas from his ecstasy and made him utter an involuntary cry. Some servants ran to the spot, but Thomas, wishing to hide the favor he had received, dismissed them courteously and kept his secret till he was on his deathbed. He then revealed it to his friend and confessor, Brother Reginald, and declared that from that time, the spirit of darkness had never been suffered to approach his person. The girdle was worn by the Saint till his death and is still preserved in the Dominican Convent of Chieri!

The virtues in men that please the Angels most are purity, humility and love of God, and these virtues were most eminent in St. Thomas.

No wonder then that he attracted the love and affection of these blessed spirits, about whom he has written so marvelously that some think that the Angels themselves came to reveal to him the secrets of their angelic natures.

It is only natural to think so since, as they are desirous of helping all their clients who call on them, they would have been much more eager to help him who has for so many reasons been called the Angelic Doctor and who labored so successfully for the Church.

ST. VINCENT FERRER

St. Vincent Ferrer, another of St. Dominic's sons, was unquestionably one of the most extraordinary Saints in the calendar of Holy Church. His life from infancy to death was one long series of prodigies, the authenticity of which rests on unimpeachable evidence. No wonder then that the Holy Angels had a special love for this great Saint, whom the Breviary calls a very portent of sanctity. On one occasion, when the Saint was entering Barcelona, he saw and spoke to the Angel Guardian of the city. This fact he announced in his sermon to the people. As a consequence, a special devotion sprang up toward the Angel, and a monument was erected in his honor. At the hour of St. Vincent's death, a multitude of the Blessed Spirits came to accompany his soul to Heaven. They filled the house in which he lay dying under the appearance of snow white birds of ravishing beauty and disappeared at the moment that the Saint breathed his last.

St. Vincent is frequently depicted with wings like an Angel.

THE FATHER SPEAKING WITH THE ANGELS

The Blessed Dalmatius was so constantly favored by the presence of his Angel that the people commonly called him the Father who speaks with the Angels. The love of the Angels for him was a fact known to all.

There are other very notable examples of Angels assisting the Dominican friars, but our space does not allow of our mentioning more.

Chapter 12

DEVOTION OF THE SISTERS OF ST. DOMINIC TO THE ANGELS

ST. ROSE OF LIMA

We have heard in the histories of many Saints that they were permitted to see and converse with their Guardian Angels. Considering the marvellous purity that distinguished Rose of St. Mary, it is no wonder that she enjoyed the privilege of constantly seeing and conversing with her Angel. Her familiarity with him was very great indeed. She talked with him *constantly*, and he attended on her and did her bidding and took messages for her. More than once when she was seriously ill, he brought her the necessary remedies at unheard-of hours. He opened the garden gate for her at night so that she could get into the house when her mother sometimes forgot to do so. Once he was seen standing by Rose's side at her cell window, both contemplating the starry heavens. They shone more brilliantly than the stars themselves. In innumerable ways he acted as her comrade and helper.

St. Rose also received frequently visits from Our Blessed Lord, who came to her in the appearance of the Divine Child, and lovingly called her "Rose of My Heart."

She grew at last to expect so certainly the gracious Infant's visits at a regular hour of the day that, if He sometimes did not appear, she felt a holy impatience, to which she often gave vent in pathetic, reproachful, or imploring verse. Once she was heard by some friends outside her cell, singing these improvised reproaches to a plaintive air, and another time a person who was standing near the hermitage just when Rose expected the Holy Child's daily visit, heard her distinctly bidding her Guardian Angel to go and remind Our Lord that the hour for His coming had passed. This she did in rhythmic language, which she intoned to a kind of sweet melancholy chant.

ST. ROSE'S MESSAGE TO THE INFANT SAVIOUR, SENT BY HER GUARDIAN ANGEL

Fly, O Swift Messenger,
Fly to Our Lord!
Oh, hasten to our Master adored!
Ask why He delays and remains
Far from our side.

Tell Him I cannot live
Parted from Him;
My life then no happiness knows:
In Him only my heart can repose
Or pleasure can find.

Fly, Noble Messenger, fly!
Tell Him when He is not here
I languish alone.
Tell Him His Rose must her sorrow bemoan
Till the moment when He shall return!

ST. AGNES OF MONTEPULCIANO

St. Agnes of Montepulciano was no less favored
by the Angels. During her life they not only appeared to her but gave her Holy Communion,
brought her relics which she had much desired
to possess and, as in the case of St. Vincent, came
to accompany her soul to Heaven.

FRANCESCA VACCHINI

In the Third Order of St. Dominic, many of
the sisters held converse with their Angels. Francesca Vacchini of Viterbo, like her namesake St.
Frances of Rome, was privileged to enjoy the constant visible protection and companionship of her
Guardian Angel. She was devoured with zeal for
souls: It seemed to be her one abiding thought.
"Father," she would constantly say to her confessor, "it seems to me there is nothing we can do
which can give God so much glory or the Angels
so much joy as to save souls; what does your Reverence think?" "Certainly," he replied.

On one occasion, she was weeping before an
image of Our Lady, when her Angel appeared
and gently reproved her for her tears. "Francesca,"

he said, "hast thou forgotten thy vocation? Hast thou not given thy heart and thy soul, thy intellect and will, yea, and thy very self into the hands of the Mother of God? Fear not, therefore, that she will ever abandon thee; it is the will of God and of His Mother that thou work for souls, and know now once again that this is the vocation which He gives thee."

Speaking familiarly with her Angel one day, as her custom was, she said, "Angelo mio, I yield to thee in every other virtue, for I know thou dost possess them more perfectly than I, and that I neither have nor can do anything, but in the matter of zeal for souls, I will not yield even to thee." "And what did your Angel reply?" said her confessor, when she related this story. "He did not reprove me as I deserved," she said, "but treated me very kindly."

The efficacy of her burning charity was known and esteemed in Heaven, and Angels appeared, lovingly contending with each other for her prayers, one moving her to say a *"Salve"* for such a soul, another suggesting the needs of a second; it was as though they made her the intercessor for their clients.

One of her beautiful visions we give at length, as a sample of many to be found in her life. "It happened that one Holy Thursday she was meditating in the church after Holy Communion, as was her custom, and lo, Our Lord Christ appeared to her under the form of a fair and comely little lamb, and suffered her to take Him into her arms and tenderly caress Him. She thanked Him with all her heart for this favor and for the marvelous spiritual sweetness which His presence gave her, but even as she held and gazed upon Him, He disappeared, leaving her sad and tearful at His departure. As she was still weeping and bemoaning her loss, her Angel spoke to her and said, "Why weepest thou, Francesca?" But she was so sorrowful for the loss of her Lord that the sight of her Angel gave her no comfort as it was wont to do, and she said, "Tell me, what sin did I commit to make Him depart from me so soon?" "Sister," replied the Angel, "it was no sin of thine that made Him depart; it happened for the benefit of the world." "Ah! my Good Angel," she answered, "I would fain know how the world could benefit by my Lord going from me!" "He came," said the Angel, "to inflame thy charity, and He departed because, had He remained, thou wouldst have been so taken up with the sweetness which His sensible presence imparted that thou wouldst altogether have forgotten those poor blind sinners for whom He would have thee live. Reflect, therefore, and consider what must be the misery of their eternal separation from God, if thou sufferest thus from the loss of His presence for a little while." And so saying, the Angel left her in peace.

Maria Raggi, a married woman and the mother of a family living in the world, was a Dominican Tertiary. Her most retired place of prayer was a corner in the public churches of Rome, and half of her life was spent in visiting the poor and serving in the hospitals. She bore the Stigmata on her venerable hands and received the crown of thorns from Our Lord Himself. She was mystically espoused to Him. Her Guardian Angel was accustomed to speak to her in an audible voice and treated her most lovingly.

Sister Laurentia Lorini was long confined to the infirmary with sickness and at first suffered much from the refusal of permission to communicate as often as she desired. But, little by little, she was observed to lose all concern about it, so that some of her Sisters even reproached her with indifference. "Sisters," she replied, "God has revealed to me through my Angel that one act of obedience is better than a thousand Communions made to please myself." Her Angel, who had taught her this great truth, was indeed her constant friend and consoler. "God," she said, "has given me three consolations in this sickness: the Blessed Sacrament, my good Angel and holy obedience; and He has taught me to gain rich crowns by very little things."

She was distinguished for her love of the choir, in which she assisted with such joy and modesty of demeanor that it seemed to be her paradise. And well might it be called so for her, because whilst there, she was accustomed to see, not her Sisters only, but all their Guardian Angels, who were by their sides in choir and assisted them in singing the praises of God. Once she saw the Angel of one of her sister-novices with a sad and melancholy countenance, for she was not yet professed, whilst all the others were glad and joyful. Laurentia was familiar with these Blessed Spirits, who often appeared to her, reproving and consoling her, and she therefore ventured to address him whom she saw with such a sorrowful expression, and ask him the cause of his sadness. "I am," he replied, "the Guardian Angel of this novice, your Sister, and I am sad because I see that she repents of her choice of this holy state. Even now her thoughts are all of the world and its follies." Laurentia lived to make her own profession, but died shortly afterwards. As she was lying on her deathbed, the Angels, her constant friends and companions, surrounded her couch and sang a chorus which was heard, not only by herself, but by her confessor and the nuns. This was the reward of one to whom the choir had been a paradise.

Dominica of the Cross was one to whom the dead were especially dear. She devoted herself to them as to the friends with whom she was most certain to find sympathy. After the death of her father, she felt a strong desire to learn the Office of the Dead by heart, so that she might be always interceding for his soul. Full of this thought, she tried if she could remember the first Psalm and, to her surprise, found herself able to recite the entire Office, which she had never before tried to learn, and which was supernaturally impressed on her memory. Her Guardian Angel faithfully assisted and encouraged her in her devotions for the Poor Souls and constantly gave her warning of the death of certain persons who needed her prayers. One night, as she was tranquilly asleep, she was aroused from her slumber and heard a sweet voice by her pillow, which said, "Dominica, the soul of one of the sisters of your Order has just departed in the monastery of Arras; arise and pray." Without a moment's hesitation she threw herself from her bed and repeated five *Paters* and *Aves* and a *De profundis,* with her arms extended in the form of a cross. The next morning brought news of the sister's death.

Blessed Emilia Bicchieri, the foundress of St. Margaret's Convent at Vercelli, sometimes refused permission to her subjects to drink outside of mealtime, exhorting them to offer up this trifling mortification for the souls in Purgatory in union with the thirst of Jesus on the Cross. "Give those drops of water into the hands of your Guardian Angel," she would say, "that with them he may quench the flames of Purgatory." One hot day it happened that Sister Cecilia Margaret offered her mortification according to the intentions of her superior. A little while afterwards, she died and appeared with a joyful and glorious aspect to Emilia, saying, "Mother, do you remember the glass of water which you denied me, and which I felt it so hard to give up. On the third day after my

death, my Angel came with it in his hand and,
in reward of my obedience, quenched with it the
flames which tormented me."

The Blessed Catherine de Matteis was one of
the greatest Dominican Tertiaries. She received
so many wonderful graces and privileges from
God that she was rightly compared to the Seraphic
St. Catherine of Siena, whom she closely resem-
bled in many ways.

Our Lord espoused her as He had espoused
St. Catherine, placing on her finger a precious
ring, impressing on her hands and feet and side
the marks of His five wounds, purifying her heart
and writing on it in letters of gold: **"Jesus my
hope."**

Our Blessed Lady bade her become a Dominican Tertiary and gave her touching proofs of her
maternal love.

This favored child of St. Dominic enjoyed fre-
quent visits of the Angels and very often conversed with them. Like St. Thomas Aquinas, she
received from them the cincture of purity, so that
her soul became as white as snow. She was also
sometimes borne by them great distances and
could see in the darkest night by the light that
shone from them. In fact, she received from the
Angels countless proofs of love and friendship.

Chapter 13

ST. FRANCES OF ROME
AND THE ANGELS

Evangelista, the beloved son of St. Frances, had been dead about a year. God gave her a sight of her dear child in Heaven and also sent him to announce to her one of the most extraordinary favors that was ever vouchsafed to a daughter of Adam. Frances was praying one morning in her oratory when she became conscious that the room was suddenly illuminated in a supernatural manner; a mysterious light shone on every side, and its radiance seemed to pervade not only her outward senses, but the inmost depths of her being, and to awaken in her soul a strange sensation of joy. She raised her eyes, and Evangelista stood before her, his familiar aspect unchanged, but his features transfigured and beaming with ineffable splendor.

By his side was another of the same height as himself, but more beautiful still. Frances' lips moved, but in vain she sought to articulate; the joy and the fear of that moment were too intense. Her son drew near to her, and with an angelic expression of love and respect, he bowed his head and saluted her. Then the mother's feelings predominated, she forgot everything but his presence and opened her arms to him; but it was no earthly form that she enclosed within them, and the ethereal body escaped her grasp. But then she gained courage and addressed him—in broken accents indeed, but with trembling eagerness.

"Is it you, indeed?" she cried, "O son of my heart! Whence do you come? Who are your companions? What your abode? Angel of God, hast thou thought of thy mother, of thy poor father? Amidst the joys of Paradise, hast thou remembered earth and its sufferings?"

Evangelista looked up to Heaven with an unutterable expression of peace and joy, and then fixing his eyes on his mother, he said, "My abode is with God; my companions are the Angels; our sole occupation the contemplation of the Divine perfections—the endless source of all happiness. Eternally united with God, we have no will but His, and our peace is as complete as His Being is infinite. He is Himself our joy, and that joy knows no limits. There are nine choirs of Angels in Heaven, and the higher orders of Angelic Spirits instruct in the Divine mysteries the less exalted intelligences. If you wish to know my place amongst them, my mother, learn that God, of His great goodness, has appointed it in the second choir of Angels, and the first hierarchy of Archangels. This, my companion, is higher than I am in rank, as he is brighter and fairer in aspect. The Divine Majesty has assigned him to you as a guardian during the remainder of your earthly pilgrimage. Night and day by your side, he will assist you in every way. Never amidst the joys of Paradise have I for an instant forgotten you, or any of my loved ones on earth. I knew you were resigned, but I also knew that your heart would rejoice at beholding me once more, and God has permitted that I should thus gladden your eyes."

God's Angel henceforward stood visibly by her side and never left her!

When Evangelista had parted from his mother, she fell prostrate on the ground and blessed God for His great mercy to her, the most worthless of sinners, for such she deemed herself; and then, turning to the Angel, who stood near her, she implored him to be her guide and director, to point out the way she was to tread, to combat with her against Satan and his ministers, and to teach her every day to become more like in spirit to his and her Lord. When she left the oratory, the Archangel followed her and, enveloped in a halo of light, remained always visible to her, though imperceptible to others. The radiance that surrounded him was so dazzling that she could seldom look upon him with a fixed gaze. At night, and in the most profound darkness, she could always write and read by the light of that supernatural brightness. Sometimes, however, when in prayer or in conference with her director or engaged in struggles with the Evil One, she was enabled to see his form with perfect distinctness. She thus described him: "His aspect is full of sweetness and majesty; his eyes are generally turned toward Heaven; words cannot describe the divine purity of that gaze. His brow is always serene; his glances kindle in the soul the flame of ardent devotion. When I look upon him, I understand the glory of the angelic nature, and the degraded condition of our own. He wears a long shining robe and over it a tunic, either as white as the lilies of the field or of the color of a red rose or of the hue of the sky when it is most deeply blue. When he walks by my side, his feet are never soiled by the mud of the streets or the dust of the road."

Frances' conduct was now directed in the most infallible manner. In her struggles with the Evil One, the Archangel became her shield of defense; the rays of light which darted from his brow sent the demons howling on their way. Thus protected, she feared neither the wiles nor the violence of Satan.

The presence of her heavenly guide was also to Frances a mirror in which she could see reflected every imperfection of her fallen, though to a great extent renewed, nature. Much as she had discerned, even from her earliest childhood, of the innate corruption of her heart, yet she often told her director that it was only since she had been continually in the presence of an Angelic Companion that she had realized its greatness — so that this divine favor, far from exalting her in her own eyes, served to maintain her in the deepest humility. When she committed the slightest fault, the Angel seemed to disappear; and it was only after she had carefully examined her conscience, discovered her failing, lamented and humbly confessed it, that he returned. On the other hand, when she was only disturbed by a doubt or a scruple, he was wont to bestow on her a kind look, which dissipated at once her uneasiness. When he spoke, she used to see his lips move and his voice was of indescribable sweetness. His guidance enlightened her chiefly with regard to the difficulty she felt in submitting to certain cares and obligations which belonged to her position as mistress and head of a family. She was apt to imagine that the hours thus employed were lost in God's sight, but her celestial guardian corrected her judgment on this point and taught her to discern the Divine Will in every little irksome worldly duty, in every trifling contradiction, as well as in great trials and on important occasions. The light of the angelic presence gave her also a marvelous insight into the thoughts of others. Their sins, their errors, their evil inclinations were supernaturally revealed to her and often caused her the keenest sorrow. She was enabled through this gift to bring back to God many a wandering soul, to frustrate bad designs, and to reconcile the most inveterate enemies. Frances used sometimes to say to Don Antonio, when she requested his permission for some additional austerities which he hesitated in granting, "Be not afraid, Father; the Archangel will not allow me to proceed too far in that course. He always checks me when I am tempted to transgress the bounds of prudence." And Don Antonio believed it, for his penitent always spoke the exact truth; and in the miraculous manner in which she ever and again read his most secret thoughts and manifested them to him, he had a pledge of her veracity, as of her extraordinary sanctity.

Saint Lydwine suffered much, but her Angel Guardian constantly appeared to her, and the vision of his beauty and his tender care filled her with happiness.

If only the sick who lie days and weeks in bed all alone were taught to feel the presence by their sides of their Angels, it would bring them immense relief.

No doctor, no nurse, no friend has the power to do for us what our Angels may do.

ST. STANISLAUS RECEIVES COMMUNION FROM AN ANGEL

The Saint lay dying in the house of a fanatical Protestant, where he had been constrained to lodge, much against his will.

He earnestly begged for Holy Communion, but both his tutor and brother were afraid to ask a priest to bring the Blessed Sacrament to this house.

St. Stanislaus then had recourse to prayer and earnestly begged St. Barbara, to whom he was much devoted, to obtain for him this great grace.

One night his tutor, Bilinski, was watching by his bedside, fearing that he might die at any moment, when he suddenly observed his countenance light up with a heavenly glow and assume an expression of mingled sweetness and reverence. But scarcely had he time to marvel at the change, when his wonder was increased by Stanislaus' turning his eyes toward him and saying in a clear and distinct voice: "Kneel and adore the Blessed Sacrament. Two Angels of the Lord are with it, and the Virgin-Martyr, St. Barbara."

"I know and am certain," said Bilinski, relating what he had witnessed, "that Stanislaus had at that time the perfect use of all his faculties, which indeed he preserved during the whole course of his illness."

As soon as he had spoken, his tutor saw him place himself in an attitude which manifested the veneration with which his whole soul was penetrated. All languid and exhausted as was his frame, he knelt upon the bed and, striking his breast three times, said, *"Domine non sum dignus,"* after which he raised his face, as in the act of receiving his Lord in the Adorable Sacrament. Bilinski looked on with awe, beholding as it were the reflection of what was miraculously passing, for his own eyes were sealed to the vision. Stanislaus then lay down again in bed, and there he remained, all absorbed in the Presence of Him whom he possessed with him.

St. Stanislaus himself confirmed this account afterwards when in Rome: "Know," he said to a fellow novice, "that having fallen ill when at Vienna in Austria, in the house of a heretic, and desiring ardently to receive Communion, I recommended myself devoutly to Saint Barbara, and while my heart continued to be filled with this desire, two Angels appeared to me in the room and with them the holy Martyr, and one of the Angels gave me Communion."

Having thus spoken, he drew a deep sigh, and his whole face was suffused with so vivid a blush that, observing it, the novice did not venture to press him with any further questions.

On another occasion, when Stanislaus was travelling on foot through Germany to Rome, he saw open a church that had once been Catholic and saw that devotions were going on. He entered but was horrified to see that the church was now in the hands of the heretics.

He was bitterly grieved, but his sadness was soon changed into joy when to his delight he saw a group of Angels coming toward him and one holding a Sacred Host in his fingers. Stanislaus fell on his knees, his heart burning with love, and received Holy Communion from the Angel.

ST. ISIDORE THE FARMER

St. Isidore was a farmer who lived and worked as a laborer in the fields near Madrid. He was accustomed before going to work to hear daily Mass. Some meddlesome people complained to the gentleman by whom he was employed that he gave his time to prayer and neglected his work.

His employer, however, had no reason to complain, as Isidore's work was well done. Nevertheless, he went to see for himself and perceived from a distance the yoke of oxen ploughing the land, led by a man whom he thought to be Isidore. On approaching nearer, he now saw that not a man but an Angel guided the oxen. It was Isidore's Angel Guardian who took his place.

ST. FRANCIS OF ASSISI

The seraphic St. Francis had a great devotion to the Angels. Some time before his death he made a forty-day fast and prayer on Mount Alvernia in honor of St. Michael. Great was his reward. One day, when he was pouring forth ardent prayers, he saw a glorious Seraph fly from Heaven to the place where he was and perceived that the Seraph was as Jesus Christ with his hands and feet extended and nailed to a cross. Beams of light flashed from his five wounds to the hands and feet and side of St. Francis, leaving on them the marks of Christ's sacred wounds, which remained indelibly on the Saint until death.

This extraordinary fact is so certain that the Church commemorates it by a special feast.

The dear St. Francis de Sales converted immense numbers of the most hardened sinners. Before beginning his sermons, he was wont to pause and look round on his listeners for some minutes.

Asked by some of his priests why he did so, he replied that he was addressing himself to the Angel Guardians of those present and begging them to take his words straight to the hearts of their clients.

This custom enabled the Saint to convert thousands of misguided and wicked heretics.

It is a custom that we all should put in practice of praying to the Angel Guardians of our enemies and those hostile to us—to prevent them from doing us injury—and to the Angel Guardians of our friends to help them and keep them from all evil.

St. Raymond of Nonnatus, when dying, eagerly desired to receive Holy Communion and feared that he might die without this last great grace, because there was no priest present. His soul was filled with joy when Angels appeared robed in the habit of his Order and gave him Holy Communion.

St. Nicolas of Tolentino heard for six whole months before his death Angels singing around his bed.

Certain it is that the dear Angels are our best and most powerful friends and repay our devotion to them a thousand times over.

In the South of France a beautiful custom formerly prevailed of saluting the Angel Guardian of everyone a person greeted: *"Bonjour Monsieur et votre cher Compagnon."* ("Good day, Sir, and your dear companion.")

This, too, we may imitate when passing people in the streets. Each one is accompanied by his Angel, and thus we meet as many Angels as we meet men and women. It is a beautiful custom to salute all the Angels we meet. They will hear our salutation most lovingly and return it most graciously.

Chapter 14

THE ANGELS HELP US ALL

We must not for a moment think that the Angels dispense their love and care only to Martyrs and Saints; they help us all and in a thousand different ways, though we may not recognize that our help comes from them. We shall mention a few instances of their loving help, accorded to ordinary mortals like ourselves.

MARSHAL TILLY

We have an authentic account of how Marshal Tilly's Angel Guardian took his place when he was hearing Mass.

During the campaign of 1663, the Marshal was assisting at Mass when Baron Lindela hastened to his side and told him that the Duke of Brunswick was about to attack the imperial army. Tilly, full of faith, bade him return at once and prepare the army for the attack, promising that he himself would join him at the conclusion of the Mass.

Before his arrival, however, the armies had met and fought fiercely, with the result that the enemy forces were utterly routed.

The Marshal, eager to know what had happened

and to which of his officers such glorious success was due, asked the Baron to whom they owed the victory. "Why," Lindela replied, "it was you your-self who led us to victory. Your appearance and personal bravery gave our men unwonted cour-age; you did wonders."

"Dear Baron," answered the Marshal, "I have been all this time at Mass. It is only this moment that I have arrived. I took no part in the battle."

"Then, dear Marshal, it was your Angel who took your place and took your appearance, for we were all persuaded that it was you yourself."

This proved to be the unanimous conviction of both officers and men.

This incident will not surprise us if we remem-ber what the Sacred Scripture tells us, *viz.*, how Machabeus was helped by five Angels. When he was in the heat of battle with his enemies, there appeared five men on horseback come from Heaven, comely and with golden bridles, leading the Jews. Two of them took Machabeus between them, covering him on every side with their arms and kept him safe, but cast darts and fireballs at the enemy, so that these fell down confounded with blindness and filled with fear. Twenty thou-sand five hundred were slain and six hundred horsemen. (*2 Machabees* 10:29-31).

Francis Albert in his work on the Angel Guar-dians tells how a Jesuit Father on his arrival in Consentia, a town in Calabria, was asked by a man to hear without delay his general confession.

He asked the reason for such haste, as the man was not ill, nor was there any other apparent reason to account for his urgent request.

The penitent told him that some time previously he and a friend of his had planned to kill another man. On the day marked for the crime, he went home and armed himself and thence proceeded to the place of rendezvous. On his way, he was unexpectedly accosted by a young man of striking appearance, who demanded in a severe tone why he was armed?

He gave a false excuse, but his interrogator replied: "Think not that you can deceive me and think not that I will look on with indifference at your taking the life of that man. You complain of a trifling offense he gave you, and you do not think of the grave offenses you have committed against God, who has saved you from eternal perdition. Make a general confession of all your sins at once and change your life. He told me of your arrival, and so I came."

Of course that young man was an Angel of God, for when he had finished speaking to the would-be criminal, he disappeared.

From this we learn how dangerous it is for us to speak ill or do harm to anyone, for without any doubt the Angel Guardian of that person will demand vengeance from God and the evil-doer will certainly be punished.

Our Lord Himself has warned us to beware lest we scandalize or harm even children, for their Angels see the face of God.

A Dominican Father told the writer that he him-self had been the recipient of many favors from his Angel Guardian.

During his childhood his good Catholic mother instilled constantly into his mind a deep and trust-ing love for his Angel. When fears and doubts assail him he instinctively has recourse to his angelic friend.

On one occasion, when a boy of nine, he was returning home at nightfall to his father's house. He had to traverse a forest, and his home was five miles distant.

When darkness came on, he became afraid and hastened his steps, but his Angel was with him.

Suddenly, he felt a wish to sit down and this without any apparent reason, for he was not at all tired, but rather desirous of getting home as quickly as possible. However, he knew not why; he did sit down under a tree.

Scarcely had he done so when he heard heavy and hasty footsteps and espied a man of forbid-ding aspect approaching. He hid himself as best he could, and the man passed on. Not many minutes after, he heard other footsteps and saw a second man of equally repulsive appearance drawing near. Once more he tried to avoid being seen and happily escaped notice.

When the two men were at a safe distance, he started at a run for home and told his father what had happened.

Next morning, news reached the family that these two men had committed a horrible murder, and all recognized the interference of an Angel in shielding their son from possibly a like fate.

On a second occasion, Father Joseph, now advanced in years, was about to set out on a journey by train. Everything was ready for departure when he felt an unaccountable desire to defer the journey. He tried to shake the thought off, but finally yielded and remained at home.

Hours later, news came that the train was derailed, with the result that twenty passengers were killed and several others wounded.

Later on in life he had a similar experience. Ready to leave home on a distant journey, this time in the company of some friends, he again for no apparent reason induced his friends to defer their departure.

Once more he and his friends learned that a dreadful accident happened to the train in which they had decided to travel, and forty passengers were killed.

THE BEAUTIFUL LANTERN

An English family had their country house on the edge of a great plain, or moor. From the windows of the house, the distant hills and forests could easily be seen. Their little boy became anxious to go and see these distant hills and trees, but his nurse told him that it was not safe.

One evening, when she was busily engaged, John availed himself of the opportunity, hastily put on his overcoat and started for the hills.

He walked until he was well-nigh exhausted. Night set in and rain fell in torrents, and little John lost his way. He was soon wet and cold and so tired that he sat down by the roadside, very frightened, not knowing what to do.

Suddenly, to his great joy, a boy appeared carrying a lantern, such a beautiful lantern as John had never seen before.

Running to meet the young man, he cried, "O please, Sir, will you show me how to get home. I have lost my way."

The young man smiled sweetly and took him by the hand. John felt ever so happy. He no longer felt cold or wet or frightened. He walked with the nice young man, admiring the wonderful lantern and chatting as they went along.

Soon they saw a house with lights in the windows. It was John's house. How did they come so quickly? But lo, the young man had disappeared!

John, delighted to be safe at home, ran up the steps and into the open hall and fell into his mother's arms.

In answer to the eager inquiries of his parents, he told them all that had happened, how he got lost and then saw the man with such a beautiful lantern, who took him by the hand and brought him home so quickly.

And when his father asked, "But why did you not ask him to come in and see us? I should have liked to thank him and offer him some recompense," the boy replied, "O, Father, when I looked for him he was gone!"

HOW DID HE ESCAPE?

A gentleman and his children were invited to a party in a friend's house. While the grown-ups were playing bridge and chatting in groups, the children romped about the house, amusing themselves as best they could.

Some of them played at sliding down the banisters. They went up to the fourth floor; that is as high as they could go. One of the group lost his balance and was thrown over the rail. As a natural result, he should have fallen to the ground floor—a height of sixty feet—and been killed. Instead, he was in some strange way thrown to the next landing. No one could see how this happened.

Stranger still, no trace of hurt or injury was found on the boy. It seemed clearly due to angelic intervention.

The End

***If you have enjoyed this book, consider making your next
selection from among the following . . .***

Ven. Jacinta Marto of Fatima. *Cirrincione* 1.50
Reign of Christ the King. *Davies* 1.25
St. Teresa of Ávila. *William Thomas Walsh* 18.00
Isabella of Spain—The Last Crusader. *Wm. T. Walsh* 20.00
Characters of the Inquisition. *Wm. T. Walsh* 12.50
Philip II. *William Thomas Walsh.* H.B. 37.50
Blood-Drenched Altars—Cath. Comment. Hist. Mexico . . 18.00
Self-Abandonment to Divine Providence. *de Caussade* . . . 16.50
Way of the Cross. *Liguorian* 75
Way of the Cross. *Franciscan* 75
Modern Saints—Their Lives & Faces, Bk. 1. *Ann Ball* . . . 18.00
Modern Saints—Their Lives & Faces, Bk. 2. *Ann Ball* . . 20.00
Saint Michael and the Angels. *Approved Sources* 5.50
Dolorous Passion of Our Lord. *Anne C. Emmerich* 15.00
Our Lady of Fatima's Peace Plan from Heaven. Booklet. .75
Divine Favors Granted to St. Joseph. *Pere Binet* 4.00
St. Joseph Cafasso—Priest of the Gallows. *St. J. Bosco* . . 3.00
Catechism of the Council of Trent. *McHugh/Callan* 20.00
Padre Pio—The Stigmatist. *Fr. Charles Carty* 13.50
Why Squander Illness? *Frs. Rumble & Carty* 2.00
Fatima—The Great Sign. *Francis Johnston* 7.00
Heliotropium—Conformity of Human Will to Divine 11.00
Charity for the Suffering Souls. *Fr. John Nageleisen* 15.00
Devotion to the Sacred Heart of Jesus. *Verheylezoon* 13.00
Sermons on Prayer. *St. Francis de Sales* 3.50
Sermons on Our Lady. *St. Francis de Sales* 9.00
Sermons for Lent. *St. Francis de Sales* 10.00
Fundamentals of Catholic Dogma. *Ott* 20.00
Litany of the Blessed Virgin Mary. (100 cards) 5.00
Who Is Padre Pio? Radio Replies Press 1.50
Child's Bible History. *Knecht* 4.00
The Life of Christ. 4 Vols. H.B. *Anne C. Emmerich* 55.00
St. Anthony—The Wonder Worker of Padua. *Stoddard* . . . 4.00
The Precious Blood. *Fr. Faber* 11.00
The Holy Shroud & Four Visions. *Fr. O'Connell* 2.00
Clean Love in Courtship. *Fr. Lawrence Lovasik* 2.50
The Secret of the Rosary. *St. Louis De Montfort* 3.00
The History of Antichrist. *Rev. P. Huchede* 3.00
Where We Got the Bible. *Fr. Henry Graham* 5.00
Hidden Treasure—Holy Mass. *St. Leonard* 4.00
Imitation of the Sacred Heart of Jesus. *Fr. Arnoudt* 13.50
The Life & Glories of St. Joseph. *Edward Thompson* . . . 13.50

At your bookdealer or direct from the publisher.

Prices guaranteed through December 31, 1995.